THINKING UNION

For Barry,

In solidarity

D'Arcy Martin

THINKING UNION

ACTIVISM AND EDUCATION
IN CANADA'S LABOUR MOVEMENT

■ ■ ■

D'ARCY MARTIN

BETWEEN THE LINES
TORONTO, CANADA

■ ■ ■ ■

Published by:
Between The Lines
720 Bathurst Street, #404
Toronto, Ontario M5S 2R4
Canada

Design by Counterpunch/Linda Gustafson
Printed in Canada by union labour
Cover picture from the series *Union Pictures*, titled ``Education" by Carole Conde
and Karl Beveridge in collaboration with the CEP. The poster version won the 1994
Canadian Association for Labour Media (CALM) prize for the best union poster.
Backcover picture by Margaret Adam/Artwork

Between The Lines gratefully acknowledges financial assistance from the Canada
Council, the Canadian Heritage Ministry, the Ontario Ministry of Citizenship, Culture and Recreation, and the Ontario Arts Council.

Canadian Cataloguing in Publication Data

Martin, D'Arcy, 1947–
 Thinking union : activism and education in
Canada's labour movement

Includes bibliographical references.
ISBN 0-921284-96-9

1. Trade-unions – Canada. 2. Working class –
Education – Canada. 3. Trade-union democracy –
Canada. I. Title.

HD6527.M37 1995   331.88'0971   C95-932233-7

Dedicated to

Mary and Hubert Martin,
teachers of dignity and caring

and

Danielle and Nyranne,
Barb, Catherine and Anita,
in solidarity

CONTENTS

. . . .

ACKNOWLEDGEMENTS

■ ■ ■ ■

Work on this book began in 1988 and in the years since has been squeezed into evenings, weekends, and vacations. Along the way many people helped me to shape and complete the writing process.

First are those who helped me to find a place in the labour movement, namely Gérard Docquier and Fred Pomeroy. My big break came when Gérard Docquier hired me into the Steelworkers, and despite a major split in the mid-1980s we have worked well together again in recent years. I hope this text conveys my continuing respect and affection for that union, and for the many honest, dedicated, and intelligent activists within it. I was particularly moved by the union leadership's decision to purchase copies of this book in advance, without seeking to influence the manuscript in any way. Fred Pomeroy hired me in 1986 and has given me space and direction in the years since. He has shown how democratic education can be respected and supported fully by a union's elected leadership. Now that he is president of the CEP, no doubt any ruffled feathers among the book's readers will be brought to his attention. I hope he continues to find my voice, while sometimes inconvenient, worthy of his support.

Three people helped me to formulate my ideas in ways that earned an Ed.D. degree from the University of Toronto: Alan Thomas, David Livingstone, and Virginia Griffin. Inspiration in that academic path came also from Rick Williams, Budd Hall, Jennifer Palin, and Judith Marshall. Those readers who are interested in a more theoretical and lengthy version of this book are invited to read the thesis "Street Smart: Learning in the Union Culture," completed in 1994.

This text would never have been completed without the steady prodding and support of Jamie Swift. As an established writer, he continually told me that I had something worth publishing and coached me in detail on the voice and stance that might get my message across on paper. With the support of the BTL staff, I secured some funding support over the years, from the Toronto Arts Council, the Ontario Arts Council, and the Canada Council. This helped me buy the time to write during my unpaid leaves of absence from the labour movement. My editor, Robert Clarke, deftly helped me to make assumptions explicit, to cut abstract rhetoric, and to be concise without being cryptic. I and the readers owe him a great deal. The combination of progressive politics and technical skill in all these Between the Lines people, whether staff, contract people, or volunteers, has stretched me without straining me. Hats off to them.

Many friends have provided comments on parts of the text. Excerpts from some of their remarks are to be found at the end of the book. Among those whose help shows more in the text itself are Jorge Garcia-Orgales, Catherine Macleod, Barb Thomas, Kate Braid, Jamie Swift, and Don Posnick. On the visual side, I thank for help and encouragement friends like Deb Barndt, Karl Beveridge, Carole Condé, Jude Johnson, Rosemary Donegan, and the late dian marino. The efforts of designer Linda Gustafson have greatly enhanced the text.

Any errors, omissions, and excesses in this book are my responsibility.

The author's royalties from sales will be used first to pay rights for the poetry and visual material reproduced here. Subsequent royalties will be donated to the Ontario Workers Arts and Heritage Centre and the Doris Marshall Institute for Education and Action.

THINKING UNION

*The author being arrested on the Radio Shack
picket line, Barrie, Ontario, August 27, 1979.*

ONE

"WE SHALL TAKE OUR FREEDOM AND DANCE"*

■ ■ ■ ■

Once, when a primary school teacher asked my daughter Nyranne to describe her father's work, Nyranne replied, "He teaches workers how to talk back." In all my years working with trade unions – and given that workers have taught me a thing or two about speaking out and hanging tough – I don't think I've ever had a better job description.

Talking back: On the morning of August 27, 1979, I was in the basement cell of the police station in Barrie, Ontario, after five of us, Steelworkers from the Toronto area, had been picked off the Radio Shack picket line by edgy, overanxious police.

We had gone to Barrie to join some women warehouse workers in their battle against the huge, Texas-based Tandy Corporation, which was ploughing its profits from the Vietnam War into consumer electronics. No Tandy location in the world was unionized, and the company had made clear that there would be no union at its Radio Shack warehouse in Barrie. There were the usual threats that the company would pull out of the city if the employees voted the Steelworkers in.

On the picket line that day I had kicked a car as it slowly moved past me to cross the line, and I now found myself charged with obstructing

* Lillian Allen. Sentence handwritten on the cover of her album *Revolutionary Tea Party* (Toronto: Verse to Vinyl, 1986) after her performance of dub poetry at Harbourfront, as part of the 1986 Mayworks Festival of Working People and the Arts.

Horace Singh, now a staff representative with the United Steelworkers of America.

police. One by one we were taken from the cell for fingerprinting, and when my turn came the constable who checked my I.D. asked what my job was. He wrote down my answer and told me I was the highest ranking of the five people arrested. Another constable yelled out, "Hey, we got ourselves the head nigger!"

I was duly given a date for a court appearance and released, but the constable's phrase kept echoing in my head. I had only been in the union's employment for a year and a half, and this contempt for both unions and black people left me feeling helpless as well as angry.

Back at the union office I got a call from the union's Ontario director. He congratulated me on my arrest, joking that now I had really completed the entrance exams into the labour move-

ment. When the case finally made it to court, the union's legal counsel advised me to dress well and emphasize my credentials as an educator who had only recently joined the union. I followed instructions, was acquitted, and the "head nigger" phrase began to fade in my memory.

The Crown appealed my acquittal, and in this new stage I realized that the local Barrie establishment was bending to Tandy's threats about pulling out of the city to avoid unionization. A conviction would help show the city's support for the company. I decided to at least score a couple of points on the way down. At that stage of the battle – it would be months before the union won the right to represent the Radio Shack workers – any gesture of defiance could help keep spirits up. When we prepared for the court appearance I asked my lawyer to be sure to question me in court about my experience in the police station after I had been arrested.

During that second set of hearings I sat in the courtroom while Horace Singh, a black Steelworker, testified about my actions on the picket line. Horace later became active as a course leader, conducting steward schools with me all over Ontario, and went on to join the Steelworker staff, servicing Toronto locals. He also now sits on the executive board of the Labour Council of Metropolitan Toronto and York Region. That day he told the court that the police had been aggressive, that the rights of picketers were not respected, and that a single kick at a car with a soft-soled shoe was not a particularly excessive expression of frustration on the line.

When I took my turn on the stand my lawyer slowly worked his way around to the events in the police station. When I mentioned the comment – "Hey, we got ourselves the head nigger" – the judge momentarily flushed, then took my lawyer to task for introducing what he considered to be "irrelevant" and "provocative" information. The judge was clearly ill at ease, and the police in the room were squirming. I looked over at Horace, and saw a smile on his face. He understood what was happening. He knew what I was trying to do.

Between the first and second set of hearings, a balance had shifted within me, from educator to union educator. My allies were workers on a picket line, and one of them was black. The episode was a moment when speaking out against racism and classism in the justice system became concretely possible. Although I do not come from the working class, I had come to know which side I was on. This time I was convicted, left with a suspended sentence and a criminal record, but for me it was an important lesson about talking back, about solidarity, about taking risks.

■ ■ ■ ■

Early in the process of writing this text, I showed a draft chapter to my friend and colleague, Paul Keighley. He returned it with a number of useful suggestions, and a note across the top: "What gives you the right to draw back from our situation and write about it?" The question rattled me, triggering a whole set of insecurities.

My initial impulse was to "sell" the project based on the needs of the labour movement and the adult education field. Certainly I hope that union activists and grassroots educators will find some encouragement and insight in the text. My second, and perhaps more realistic, response was to assert my personal need and right to speak. Union education is central to my life, and I have a creative urge, a passionate desire to talk about it. I am convinced that union education has the potential to change power relations in the workplace and in the society more broadly. I want to share what I have learned in years of facilitating other people's learning, from picket lines at dawn to contract ratification meetings in the late evening. It would be dishonest to present my motivation only as social service. In this text is a calm, defiant message to those with whom and against whom I have struggled over the years: I won't opt out, I won't be pushed out, and I won't be silenced.

Yet my voice is only one in labour's internal discussions, and in some respects it is an unusual one. Most union staff come from within the membership, rather than being hired from outside as I was in 1978. My upbringing was in a "red Tory" family, settled as lawyers for generations in the industrial city of Hamilton, with a strong tradition of community service. My schooling was in well-run private boys schools, which instilled a strong achievement drive. My undergraduate involvement in the student movement of the late 1960s anchored a personal conviction that education can and should be part of a broad popular movement for social and political change. My exposure to the politics and culture of Latin America, through travel there and work with refugees here, radicalized my understanding of how power works.

I have since met many people with that special combination of spirit and skill that it takes to challenge authority carefully and creatively, and I continue to learn with them. Along the way I have shared some of my book smarts and absorbed some of their street smarts. This book grows from dialogue, distilled from a floating conversation in a range of places over many years. I draw it together at a time when many people are discouraged about the prospects for transforming power relations in this country.

■ ■ ■ ■

A couple of years after the incident in Barrie I was in Ottawa with Danielle, the older of my two daughters.

Danielle had been three when I started work in the labour movement. For her, in a world of things you could touch, "the union" that kept me away from home so much was a puzzling thing. It was hard to get ahold of. When she came to my office, she would ask if it was the union. I would say no, the office was a support to the union, but the union was not a place. When she came to courses or meetings, she would ask if this was the union. I would answer no, education was just one of the ways to build the union. When we drove past the steel plants in Hamilton, she would ask if the factories were the union. Again I would have to say no, the plants were places where union members worked. All these things and places were connected to the union, but the union itself was a relation among people.

In Ottawa in November 1981 Danielle was six years old, and we were walking from a car park to join a demonstration against high interest rates on Parliament Hill. I was tired after the drive from Toronto to Ottawa and wasn't too happy about her insistence that I carry her. She was heavy on my shoulders, and her boots were digging into my ribs as I lurched around the corner onto Wellington Street, ready to see a normal turnout on a chilly Saturday. Then I stopped short. We saw a huge mass of people on the lawn outside the Parliament Buildings – the largest crowd I had ever seen in Canada (estimated later at a hundred thousand people) – and the sight took my breath away. I felt Danielle bounce forward on my shoulders, and suddenly her nose was almost touching mine. "Papi, this must be the union." I squeezed her ankles happily, and said yes, it was.

Nyranne Michelle Shilton Martin (left) and Danielle Alexa Shilton Martin, 1982.

That kind of exhilaration is not always the case. The union for me has also meant fatigue, loneliness, and disappointment. I have seen good ideas destroyed by personal feuds, and dedicated people discouraged when they couldn't halt an inequity, a firing, or a plant closure. I have felt overwhelmed by the range and intensity of learning needs among workers, and the great difficulties of working to try to meet those needs. At times the same callousness and egotism we see in management show up inside the union, where they are even more upsetting because of the lofty principles promoted by the movement.

Still, when I become weary, tempted to move into a quieter harbour of the adult education field, moments like the courtroom in Barrie and the march in Ottawa come back into my mind, lightning flashes of clarity in the mist of everyday work. I see a strong, unified labour movement, willing to fight the employers and the state on issues that affect all Canadian workers; a movement based on collective, enlightened self-interest; a movement that knows how to struggle and how to create. I am one of many people trying to build this elusive concept of a "union" inside the always imperfect institutions of our society.

■ ■ ■ ■

The record of union activism in Canada has been transmitted from one generation to another mostly by stories, shared informally. Union work puts me in a continuous dialogue with working people about how their workplaces, communities, and unions function – what is good, what is bad, and what could be better shaped to their needs. My work gives me pleasure. There is daily challenge in:

> work of the speaker who also listens
> meticulous delicate work of reaching the heart of the desperate woman, the desperate man
> – never-to-be-finished, still unbegun work of repair.[1]

The range and pace of situations that I have worked in have been dizzying. I entered the labour movement early in the period 1975–89, which has been defined as "the counter-attack," the effort of employers and governments to weaken unions permanently.[2] Those years included wage controls (1975–78), a depression (1981–84), and the Mulroney government's neoconservative package of privatization, deregulation, and free trade (1984–89) – and since then an ongoing "jobless recovery." Throughout this period the labour movement was subject to economic and political attack. Unions were kept on the defensive, and the establishment had the whip hand economically and politically.[3]

As part of these battles, by the early 1980s the labour movement began to have an increased understanding of the potential value of coalitions. Educators and activists facing the New Right and unionists facing the same neo-conservative agenda began to get together in increased communication and mutual assistance. The political and economic offensive against labour extended into the educational life of the movement, as one would expect. The challenge of union educators and our allies, then, was to reintegrate socialist insights into the thoughts of workers.

Despite the setbacks, trade unions in Canada have been on the move. In the early 1960s, for instance, about 30 per cent of non-agricultural workers in both Canada and the United States belonged to unions. By 1986 the share in the United States had dropped to 19 per cent while the Canadian figure had increased to 39 per cent. By 1994 the figures stood at 14 per cent for the United States and 36 per cent for Canada. In other words, the Canadian movement now has proportionately more than double the social presence of its counterparts to the south.[4]

This dynamism has affected all aspects of labour relations, including membership education. On October 14, 1976, a million workers stayed off

With the CEP delegation at the May 15, 1993 march on Parliament Hill are Bob White, president of the Canadian Labour Congress, and Nancy Riche, executive vice-president.

the job in protest against wage and price controls, the largest general strike in Canadian history. Then in 1981 came the demonstration on Parliament Hill to protest the federal economic policies that were engineering a depression – a hundred thousand people led by the labour movement. During the 1988 federal election, labour's public profile grew in an unprecedented fashion in the campaigns against the free trade agreement. Subsequently, in coalition with churches, women's groups, and other social allies, labour has evolved a program of action to resist the New Right, focused on the Action Canada Network. A march on Ottawa on May 15, 1993, once again brought hundreds of thousands of unionists into the streets.

During my days with the United Steelworkers of America (USWA), from 1978 to 1986, I seemed to be constantly coming up against new challenges – I call the various stages "initiation time," "coming to terms," and "civil war time." Later, when I moved to the Communications and Electrical Workers of Canada (CWC), I had to apply what I had learned about education in a very different union. In 1992 the CWC joined with two other unions of roughly equal size to create the Communications, Energy and Paperworkers Union of Canada (CEP). In this new union, fourth largest in the private sector in Canada, I remain as education representative for the Ontario Region.

By the mid-1990s, conditions in the labour movement had altered dramatically from what they had been when I first started in the late 1970s – in the politics of gender and race especially, but also in shifting patterns of employment, in the impact of new technology, and in the nature and scope of trade union organizations. Teaching workers how to talk back to power has become a more fluid, diverse, and complex job.

Through these years, many changes happened around me. I feel very much like Judy Darcy, who has observed:

> That's been one of the most exciting aspects of union life for me, see-ing the changes in workers who were given a chance to develop skills, build confidence, and actually become different people. It's the same kind of developmental change that happens to people on a picket line, for as we know a strike is an educational experience like no other. How the labour movement develops its activists and leaders and enriches their lives is still the aspect of unionism that people under-stand the least.[5]

The changes within me have been harder to chart. The demands of the work have strained me and damaged my links with family and friends. Still, along the way I have paused to think, particularly in three study leaves. In 1984–85 I took ten months away from the Steelworkers to study adult education theory. In 1988–89 a leave from the CWC allowed me to read and travel. In 1992–93 a voluntary leave from the CEP allowed me to complete the Ed.D. thesis on which this book is based.[6]

For six years my union, the CWC, used the slogan "Thinking Union" in its education programs. The phrase expressed a collective recognition that unionists have to exercise certain powers of logical thought, judgement, and creative imagination if they are going to advance the values and needs of working people. The phrase also expressed a collective decision to help members develop a "union mindset" and to support leaders in adapting unionism to new needs and pressures.

This book explores hopes and strategies within that "union mindset." It is aimed at "conscious romantics" – people who dream of a better world and know the obstacles in the way of building it. I first heard this phrase from a friend of mine, Richard Swift, when he was interviewing me for a radio program. After I had come out with one of my more optimistic remarks Richard said, "Oh D'Arcy, you're such a romantic. Well, with what you've gone through I guess you're a *conscious romantic.*" Since then I've come to believe that conscious romantics are found in many parts of the worldwide social justice movement, comparing notes, sharing stories, nourishing one another against the siren songs of cynicism, challenging the power structures, while all the while trying to keep our own disappointments to a minimum. For readers from inside the labour movement, I hope the book will trigger key points in your own learning. For those looking in from outside, I hope it will add to your understanding of the particular beauty and pain of union life.

I especially hope that this book will encourage other unionists to raise their voices, to go on record themselves . . . in protest against the injustices around us and in singing the praises of the movement we are helping to build:

> We sing because shouting is not enough
> nor is sorrow or anger
> we sing because we believe in people
> and we shall overcome these defeats
>
> we sing because the sun recognizes us
> and the fields smell of spring
> and because in this stem and that fruit
> every question has its answer
>
> we sing because it is raining on the furrow
> and we are the militants of life
> and because we cannot and will not
> allow our song to become ashes.[7]

TWO

INITIATION TIME

■　■　■　■

If only I were a better speaker
If only I knew more facts
If only I'd changed my shirt

If only I knew what they were thinking
Maybe they're thinking what I'm thinking
Maybe we're all thinking the same thing
And everybody is just waiting for someone else to say it
Someone else to spit it out
Someone like me.

Why me?

— Steven Bush, *Life on the Line*

When I first started work at the United Steelworkers of America, the union seemed powerful and haphazard, and highly confusing. In time I came to see things differently, but first impressions from the interview, followed two weeks later by my first morning on the job, threw me strangely off balance.

I arrived early for the interview and spent twenty increasingly nervous minutes outside the office of the national director as strangers hurried purposefully past. These people worked there and had what I wanted

– a job with the Steelworkers – but for now they left me feeling smaller and smaller.

Gérard Docquier, who had been recently elected the Steelworkers' national director for Canada, greeted me by asking, "Are you the one who doesn't want to travel?"

"Well," I said, "I don't want to be on the road all the time. I've got a young family."

"The job is on the road. But come on in."

We spoke for a few minutes about my adult education experience and the union's need to support representatives in the workplace. Then out of nowhere came: "What are your plans, anyway? We know you academics. You stay with a union a couple of years, put that experience on your résumé, and move to a government policy job."

I told Gérard I had already turned down a couple of offers for government

Gérard Docquier, in his initial election campaign for National Director, United Steelworkers of America.

jobs, so that wasn't a goal for me. I said I planned to commit myself to the Steelworkers for five years and that I would want an unpaid year off after that to study. "Before the study leave I'll commit as to whether I'm coming back," I said. Then I took a bit of a leap. "If you try to get rid of me in less than five years I'll grieve the dismissal, and if I lose the grievance I'll go public."

He grunted and said, "It's good you don't expect to be paid during your study leave."

That was my introduction to the Steelworkers, and to Gérard Docquier's emotionally blunt way of handling relations with his staff. Looking back, I'm sure I got the job partly because I showed a willingness to stand up for myself. Also, the other National Office staff had supported Docquier's opponent, Don Taylor, in recent elections for the position of national director, so it was perhaps understandable that Docquier decided to go outside the union for his first hiring. As a Québécois, Gérard also may have wanted me because I spoke French.

The next time I showed up at Gérard's door, this time to start work, I was greeted more warmly. Jocelyne Sévigny, Gérard's right arm, helped me through some paperwork about hiring, then took me in to see Gérard.

He seemed distracted as he wished me luck. We were both relieved by a knock on the door. A head popped in, and the head said, "Excuse me, I just need to get a chair for the new guy."

"Actually, James, this is the new guy. His name is D'Arcy Martin. So, D'Arcy, what about the chair you're sitting in right now?" Gérard sounded both imperious and anxious. "It feels fine," I mumbled, and I returned their smiles, tentatively. Gérard smiled broadly now. "Then take it with you to your office."

I picked it up and followed James Peters down the corridor. I was to spend eight years walking back and forth to Gérard Docquier's office. Still today, when I meet with him in his role as labour co-chair of the Canadian Labour Force Development Board, I remember the mixture of confusion and bravado I felt that first day.

At the time little of the Steelworker style and even less of its office politics made much sense to me. The afternoon before I had finished up at the Development Education Centre (DEC), where I had worked for the past six years. Since 1972 four of us – Jonathan Forbes, Dinah Boulton Forbes, Anita Shilton Martin, and myself – had worked at building up DEC into a cohesive small collective of adult educators who produced and diffused learning materials about the Third World. At the start we were mostly engaged in writing and doing workshops for high school teachers, but by the time I left DEC the organization had grown to fourteen staff members doing educational work and running a bookstore, library, and film distribution service, as well as producing slide-tape shows, radio programs, books and pamphlets, and a documentary film – all centred around issues of underdevelopment in Canada as well as the international power system.

At DEC we kept in touch with unionists, especially those interested in international solidarity work, and that's how I first heard about the Steelworkers' opening for a Canadian education director. Gower Markle had been in the job for over twenty years and was about to move on to Labour Canada, where he would administer the grants for union education that so greatly increased the Canadian Labour Congress's education capacity. I had decided that it was time to leave DEC and sent the Steelworkers a formal letter of application. It was seven months before I received a note acknowledging my application, but meanwhile my friends Peter Warrian and Michel Blondin, both on the Steelworker staff, informally encouraged me to wait. I had known Peter Warrian since 1967, when we met as part of the Canadian student movement. I had met Michel Blondin in Bolivia in 1971, and we'd found that we shared a strong interest in popular education and international solidarity. As education representative for the Steelworkers in Quebec, he had turned down the offer to move to Toronto as Canadian education director and encouraged me to try for it. After I finally heard formally from the union, the process speeded up. Within two weeks I was interviewed, hired, and asked to start immediately. With my head spinning, I showed up for work on March 1, 1978.

My decision to move from DEC had personal dimensions to it. One was financial. My wife Anita also worked at DEC, and our combined income was $15,000 a year. With our first daughter, Danielle, turning two, and a second child planned, one decent salary in the family seemed essential. I also wanted to move from a job with an international focus to one that would take me more deeply into issues in my own country. And I wanted to work in a larger organization with a defined social and political base.

Like most socialist intellectuals, I was convinced that unions were central to progressive politics in Canada, but it seemed that real contributions to union education could only be made from the inside. So I decided to give it a shot. And on my first day I thought I was the luckiest adult educator in the world. Looking back, I still feel that way. But the scale of the challenge was just beginning to come clear in my mind.

Nearly two hundred thousand Canadian workers belonged to the Steelworkers then, and over a million Americans. The U.S. members got their technical services – legal, health and safety, public relations, and research as well as education – from the Pittsburgh headquarters. In Canada three geographical districts got parallel support through a national office with a couple of dozen specialized staff. As one of four staff members in the Education Department, my job was to reach out to some five to ten thousand elected workplace representatives from across Canada each year. The courses, each with twenty to twenty-five participants, brought together various levels of what I would later call the union "staircase" – the elected hierarchy of unionists – from member to steward, chief steward, local union officer, local president, staff representative, and national officer.

This was not the first or the last time in my life that I felt overwhelmed by a challenge. But in hindsight my concerns seem to have been oddly misdirected. My main fear then was about screwing up technically. After all, I was twenty-two years younger than the next youngest department head in the union. I was concerned that the ongoing work of designing and facilitating learning in a large organization might be beyond my competence. As it turned out, I was able to handle that aspect of the job, but what I did have to learn was a whole new set of political skills: reading the balance of power among factions, understanding what moves people to fight, balancing the democratic and authoritarian currents within the union. These lessons were to wrench open my fears and doubts, to demand new levels of nerve and compassion.

LEARNING MOMENTS

My initiation was like learning to drive a car. At first there were many elements requiring conscious attention – shifting gears, signalling turns, watching for pedestrians and other drivers. But after a while the jumble of traffic took on predictable patterns, and a sixth sense for trouble seemed to develop. With time I learned about carefully signalling turns, and about when I should slow down.

I spent my first six months on the job listening. There was a string of meetings with local union leaders. I heard about the accomplishments and shortcomings of the past and the hopes for the future. A recurring concern was the need to revive the enthusiasm and strengthen the knowledge of the shop stewards. In each workplace, a steward would be elected to handle problems for fifteen to thirty fellow workers. Although the stewards would be trusted and/or popular in the workplace, they needed outside support to organize the flood of union information and to develop skills of effective representation. This grassroots union building had begun with Michel Blondin in the Steelworkers union in Quebec. It became the heart of my work in English Canada.[1]

I was working about sixty hours a week and travelling one week out of three to the mining and industrial towns where members lived. The richness of that period for me was outside the formal meetings and the piles of heavy reading on labour relations and contract-making that cluttered every desk at the National Office.

- In the bar of an Ottawa Valley motel, a seasoned organizer talked about snowshoeing into a mining camp in the 1950s because the company wouldn't let a Steelworker travel in on its private train line.
- Squeezed into the heated picket cabins of a Sudbury winter, strikers at International Nickel watched one of my favourite films distributed by DEC, *Controlling Interest*, and talked about their bitterness about how so little of the wealth of the multinationals had been ploughed back into their community.

▪ At lunch in a Chinese restaurant in Saskatoon, a steward explained matter-of-factly about how one of the local union officers had started a damaging rumour about a potential opponent to preserve his elected position.

▪ Joining other participants at a demanding communications course in the Laurentians, in a heartfelt and tipsy "Gens du Pays."

▪ On an early morning bus from Halifax a co-worker told how the change from irregular work on the lake boats to a steady job in the steel mill had stabilized his life.

▪ Pressing my rusty Spanish into service with a group of radical Chilean members enraged by asbestos dust blowing around their plant and suspicious that their union staff rep might be in the pocket of management.

These moments contained the themes around which I learned – fighting the companies, handling the internal politics, and relating to the lives of the members outside the union meeting. My political sympathies became grounded in personal friendships.

When it came time for me to teach as well as learn, I took off for a week-long course in Trail, B.C., to test a newly designed introductory steward manual. Everything seemed to go wrong: the airport was fogged in, my luggage was lost, and the teaching manuals and films had not arrived. Somehow I managed to "wing it" through the first day, thanks partly to my co-teacher, Tony Belcher, a talented staff rep who later left to work on the company side. Among those preparing to teach the course in the field were Emil Shumey, now with the federal government, and Ken Georgetti, now president of the British Columbia Federation of Labour.

On the third evening of the course several of us were watching hockey on TV in a hotel room. During a break in the action one of the course leaders, Bill Deline of Cassiar, British Columbia, mentioned that he needed to go home early. It turned out that his local was currently on strike and he was afraid of running out of cash before the week's end. During a commercial we passed around a hat and Bill suddenly had enough for meals and hotel and then some.

"I want everybody's name so I can pay you back after the strike is over," he blurted out, obviously overwhelmed by the gesture.

"Have a beer and stop interrupting the game!" someone yelled, and we all settled back in for the evening. Bill remained for the rest of the course and proved to have a lot of staying power: he subsequently taught many steward courses for the union, especially in the mining communities of western Canada.

This incident – far removed from the "professional" climate of formally structured adult education programs – surely had as much to do with the eventual success of the course as the study materials, which had arrived that morning. Not far into the week, steering through this solidarity seemed as familiar to me as driving a car.

After all, nobody really learns about the heart of unionism in a course. Formal union education is a chance to compare notes on the lessons of support and conflict learned through experience – on the job, in union meetings, and in the ebb and flow of internal politics. Courses are one moment in the learning process of the union culture, a moment that should be taken seriously, but not too seriously.

"BACK TO THE LOCALS"

I had joined the Steelworkers at a time of great dynamism and militancy. The union was reviving member participation, recruiting the unorganized and extending the range of action to health, equity, and other issues. The openings for conscious, radically democratic education work seemed legion.

A lot of my work began, quite routinely, with a request from a local union officer. Maybe the officer wanted a "refresher" course for experienced stewards to revive their interest and sharpen their skills or respond to a new management initiative.

If the request came, say, from the mining area around Kamloops, B.C., education rep Don Posnick in Vancouver would be on the phone to me right away. Don would propose a three-day course in the town where the request came from and find an experienced course leader from another mining area who could also attend. We would review the current policy priorities both in the union itself (technological change, or women's rights, for instance) and within the B.C. Federation of Labour (perhaps labour law, or compensation for injured workers), and we would ensure that these priorities would be addressed in a film, handout, or role play during the course. We might canvass other locals in the area to see if any members wanted to attend the session. The local's chief steward might be encouraged to attend an intensive, week-long course on grievance arbitration to ensure that the local would have enough expertise on site to guide and support the newly "refreshed" stewards after the course.

Don and I would also pore over the political subtexts of the situation both at the local and in the community. Is the request based on a motion from the local union meeting, or is it the initiative of a single officer who might want to take credit for the results? Are stewards in the local on good terms with their staff representative, or might they be trying to dodge that rep by seeking alternative advice on certain issues? Are the neighbouring locals comfortable with the incumbent officers of this local, or would they respond better if the district office "hosted" the course in a more neutral way, making sure all locals are equally encouraged to send participants? Are there municipal, provincial, or federal elections in the offing, and can the course possibly provide a forum for the area's NDP candidates? Is there resistance in the area to a union policy on environmental issues or Native rights, for instance, and if so how can we best face this resistance?

BACK TO THE LOCALS PROGRAM

This image has been carried on all Steelworkers education material in Canada since 1979, and is still in use.

Questions like these were as important as technical matters of scheduling, arranging facilities, or preparing core study materials. In a social movement, education visibly strengthens one set of ideas and people at the expense of others, and this power must be exercised in a careful, responsible way. Unions are clearly no place for politically naive or "neutral" education, nor should courses be a tool for manipulative or arbitrary leadership.

During this period two situations, one in Newfoundland and the other in Ontario, especially captured the flavour of the times. In the first one, in Baie Verte, Newfoundland, asbestos miners decided in early 1978 that they had had enough. They had known for years, long before the medical establishment was forced to admit it, that their own direct exposure to asbestos fibres would kill them. Now evidence was coming out that the fibres were damaging their children as well. A quiet, conservative community went on strike for six months, not for wages but for health. The men returned to the mine with several victories: a car wash, so their vehicles wouldn't carry fibres home from the mine; a sprinkler and shelter system, to prevent fibres being blown from the mine into the town; and a proper "dry," a change room so asbestos-laden clothes would not be taken back and blown through their own houses by the laundry machines. In this battle, all the resources of the international union were committed to supporting the strike.

In Etobicoke, Ontario, a western suburb of Toronto, workers at the Irwin Toy factory decided they needed a union. Low wages, arbitrary discipline, and insulting supervision finally provoked employees to challenge management's stand that the company would always be "union free." When enough cards had been signed, with the Steelworkers certified to represent the workers, management began a relentless campaign to break the union. As the crucial Christmas sales period approached, the union's staff rep, Alex Muselius, got dressed in a Santa Claus suit and began patrolling downtown Toronto handing out stickers saying, "Don't buy Irwin Toys." When the company met Alex across the bargaining table the next week, they hurried to reach an agreement with the union.

In the late 1970s the union was growing steadily by organizing the unorganized, so innovative ideas were being welcomed and I had a solid mandate to make changes. In 1979 the Steelworkers adopted the "back to the locals" slogan as the basis of its union education. The program was based on five core elements, which together provided a procedural architecture that would guide the development of membership education throughout my eight years with the Steelworkers.

(1) Increased and updated courses for stewards

Everywhere in the labour movement, the shop stewards are referred to as the "backbone" or "front line" of the union. Yet making them the priority for education meant reducing the resources and time spent with more senior and more influential local union officers. For me it meant putting aside "sexier" advanced courses on innovative topics in favour of a sustained focus on these grassroots activists. Supporting the stewards, in grievance handling and in keeping up membership interest and involvement became the prime focus, almost an obsession, of work for my first two years at the union. It meant producing a slide-tape show called "What Am I Getting Into?" built on interviews with active stewards across the country. It meant reorganizing logistics, bringing education to the stewards instead of vice versa.

(2) Teaching by local union course leaders

To carry a common message out, and to build participatory dynamics in the courses, a key initiative was selecting, training, and supporting course leaders from among local union activists. These part-time educators, with their anchors still solidly in their own workplaces, were the two-way channel between me and the stewards. As the momentum of the program developed, and the effect of well-trained local activists became clear after sessions like the Trail and London courses, staff increasingly associated themselves with the idea and monitored the selection and deployment of course leaders.

(3) Increasing financial support to education

Funds for each course had to be negotiated from a variety of sources. The three Canadian district offices located in Vancouver, Toronto, and Montreal generally absorbed costs of publicity and setup, while the National Office looked after facilities and instructors. The local unions covered the costs of lost wages, travel, and accommodation for participants. This diffusion of financial authority brought with it the need to win financial co-operation from the districts and locals for each and every course.

Gradually I learned how to link new initiatives with politically significant parts of the union, so that Gérard Docquier would hesitate to veto the expenditures involved. I learned to time my important initiatives to when money was available. To increase the money for education meant being politically alert, not just altering a budget line.

(4) Making locations and scheduling more accessible

Local union officers wanted courses located near the workplace, so that travel costs would be reduced and members with family responsibilities could attend more easily. It was in this sense of logistics that the phrase "back to the locals" was first used. Many of the cultural obstacles to participation were also reduced by bringing course leaders right to the local union and holding courses in the familiar terrain of the union hall.

To lessen the financial strain on smaller local unions, many courses were held on a Friday-Saturday basis, with the lost wages of participants covered on the Friday while they volunteered their time on the Saturday. Because participants were volunteering their time on Saturdays, our practice was that course leaders were also not paid for Saturday teaching unless they were missing a scheduled shift. Similarly (and painfully) it meant that education staff like myself did not get any compensation in time or money for weekend work.

(5) Co-ordinating courses

Within the union the resources that could be applied to member education were scarce. This meant that it was essential to join the efforts of the Steelworkers to those of the central labour bodies. This involved negotiating a division of labour among three levels within the Steelworkers, and three levels of central labour bodies.[2]

Steelworkers	Central Labour Bodies
▪ National Office	▪ Canadian Labour Congress
▪ District Office	▪ Federations of Labour
▪ Local Union	▪ Labour Councils

To the degree that I was able to work with the other "providers" in this picture, I could bring educational support to the activists in the workplace. If I got into turf battles, or ideological debates, I would be limited to those resources available in the National Office budget, and the whole initiative would collapse.

These five points, then, provided the initial framework for my work as a union educator. By the end of my "initiation time" in 1981, the scaffolding for this structure was in place. During my years at the Steelworkers, some points would increase in significance, while others ebbed, but the structure remained intact. I have carried this mental framework with me ever since into conversations with union educators in Canada and elsewhere. It was the main product of my "initiation time."

Much later on, in the summer of 1994, I dropped by the Steelworkers' National Office to present a copy of my doctoral thesis on union education to the union. This was long after a political clash had driven me out in 1986. Hugh Mackenzie, assistant to the national director, warmly accepted the thesis and said I was welcome at the office, for two reasons. One was that the "back to the locals" program had proved of lasting value in renewing member participation in the union. The other reason was that my work since 1986 carried the marks of my learning from the Steelworkers. He and other activists in the union could see that I was still using, and acknowledging, what they had taught me.

CATCHING STRIDE

The "closing of ranks" within a union was brought home to me early, during the Inco strike of 1978–79 in Sudbury, Ontario. In numbers of workers and duration, this was the biggest strike in Canada's labour history, and I tumbled into it during my first year as a union educator.

The Steelworker leadership in the United States and Canada had advised the membership against striking International Nickel at a time when the company had a large stockpile and prices were low. The members voted to go out, led by Dave Patterson, a populist, charismatic local union president. Throughout the strike and for years later, Patterson and the Steelworker establishment would be at each other's throats. Whoever was "right" in this case, the members settled in for a cold winter, the international settled in for a huge draw on the strike fund, and the bargaining committee settled in to try and reach an agreement.

After seven months of meetings at the Royal York Hotel in Toronto the union's bargaining committee reached a tentative deal with the company and then travelled north to take the news to the local membership in Sudbury. I remember explaining to a friend how good a deal they had reached, and how certain it was that any posturing by local stewards would be swamped in a membership acceptance vote. But the Sudbury members voted it down. They said they were damned if they were going back for so little after seven months out. I was surprised, but not nearly as shaken as the members of the bargaining committee, who were forced back to the negotiating table.

At the time there was a high degree of division and confusion in the Sudbury union hall, and one day a magazine journalist, an outsider, decided to probe the situation. When he tried to interview people just outside the main meeting room, one after another they expressed their support for the bargaining committee and the international union. In public the ranks had closed. The fight was within the family . . . a family of more than ten thousand workers, but a family nonetheless.

This took place in a group made up of a broad cross-section of nationalities, but most of them were white men, Canadian-born, and middle-aged. The elected leaders embodied their membership, and unity in the face of management came fairly spontaneously.

Later on, about three years into the job, I had a different sort of experience that also helped to define union cohesiveness for me. I was coaching eight men and three women Steelworkers in a union hall in Toronto. Warily getting to know one another and the job ahead, we began talking about shop stewards and the key role they play in the union. Everyone but me had been a steward at one time, and they were preparing to teach others what they knew. This was Monday afternoon, and a course for eighty new shop stewards had been scheduled for that weekend in London. My "train the trainer" session was preparing this group for their first formal venture as adult educators.

The novice educators were nervous. The volume of information and skills must have appeared overwhelming, and the learner-centred approach unfamiliar. I seemed to be a lightning rod for the anxieties people felt. The tension flashed on Tuesday afternoon. Dave Mellor, a miner from Elliot Lake (and now a staff representative for the United Steelworkers of America), snickered because I missed the significance of a particular contract clause. "You really don't know what it's like to fight grievances, do you?" he said. "You've never been on the shop floor like us."

This struck a little too close to my own self-doubts for a polite response, so I went on the offensive. "And you've never had your mind go blank in front of a class of twenty people," I said. "If you think you can teach the stewards on Friday in London without my help, go ahead. I can collect my salary just for sitting here until then."

Then a quieter guy spoke up with another side of the anger. "That's fine for you to say when you've had years of teaching practice," he said. "What you're asking us to do is learn all that in four days. It's impossible. We'll look like fools."

The discussion ran for about half an hour. We talked about our different experiences with teachers. I heard about how bitterly industrial unionists resent their treatment in school. Then I talked about my right to respect as well as theirs. And we acknowledged the fear of change, around us and within us.

In that conversation the façades were cracked, and we made a commitment to help one another. Then we set to work, reviewing the study resources prepared by previous teaching teams. The initial design and selection of materials had been done by a working group including myself and Tony Belcher, Wilf Hudson, Patti Jonas, and Don Posnick. We had met in Calgary for three days, cutting and pasting the best of our materials until we came up with a consensus outline for the course, including role plays, lecture notes, and instructions for operating film projectors. The participants worked late into each evening in twos and threes to become familiar with the tools.

On Thursday afternoon we were finishing up the photocopying of hand-outs when Dave Mellor pulled me aside. "It was good the way you fought back when I went after you," he said. "It's sort of crazy, but if you hadn't shown who was in charge we would have kept on coming and driven you right out the door."

Dave was as relieved by the outcome as I was, although the relief was mixed for both of us. Part of him still resented my authority. Part of me was awash with guilt, since my declared purpose had been to have them control the process, and yet at the first challenge I had fought to protect my own turf. Both of us were uneasy about the "macho clash" we had engaged in, a kind of interaction we were both trying to outgrow. But that was the best we could do at that point.

On Friday morning I opened the course with a short speech in a plenary session with the eighty new stewards. Then all the participants divided into four workshop groups, with three new "course leaders" in each. I drifted from room to room and could feel the energy in discussions, the buzz in the work groups, the ease of the leaders in responding to questions. We had arranged a short meeting of course leaders for lunchtime, to check out problems, but they were going so strongly they ignored the sandwiches and rushed to thread films and prepare flip charts for the afternoon. That evening they were exultant, and so was I. Yet I was also taken aback by the rapport they had established in their groups – a rapport I felt I could never have accomplished – precisely because they were anchored in their workplaces, just like the other participants. These were grassroots activists, outperforming professional educators.

That Saturday evening the dozen educators squeezed into a smoky hotel room, relaxing. It felt like the locker room after a winning game. One of the three women in the group was imitating the accent in an Australian-made film we had shown. People started teasing one another about our own accents. It was easy and warm in the room. As the public toasts went around, I silently toasted the end of my initiation. With a mixture of satisfaction and uneasiness, I knew that I was now part of the union, no longer a beginner.

I drove home on Sunday with a quiet, conspiratorial smile, knowing that if we could do this, so could many, many, others. The next Monday morning we were all back at work – drilling underground in Sudbury, running a punch press in Barrie, pouring moulds in Renfrew . . . and writing new role-plays at the union office in Toronto. Different jobs, different backgrounds, different skills flowing together through the union.

■ ■ ■ ■

As I settled into my union role, and dealt with my co-workers' needs and doubts as best I could, I came to see that no union activist is only just a unionist. Each of us has identities and interests beyond the role played in the labour movement. As the years went by, I came to see my own particular shape through the eyes of others. I found that four other parts of my life flowed into my union action, sometimes enriching and at other times distracting: international solidarity, educational theory, local political action, and family life. Each of them conditioned my work and each changed over the years.

First was my interest in Latin America, developed in my early twenties as a student of the politics and culture of "underdevelopment" and revolutionary change. My perspective on Canada, on learning, and on power was deeply shaped by this exposure. The ideas of radical educators like Paulo Freire affected my sense of what was possible and necessary in developing dialogue with oppressed people rather than presenting them with top-down solutions. In recent years, largely through associates in the Doris Marshall Institute, I have broadened connections with popular educators in Mexico, Central America, Southern Africa, and East Asia. Their faith in the wisdom of the oppressed, their capacity to innovate with limited resources, and their linking of education to organizing for change continue to affect me deeply.[3]

Second, there is my continuing dialogue with adult educators since I first entered the field in the late 1960s. I was initially drawn into the field by the late Roby Kidd, who said he thought a student rebel – I was then very much involved in "student power" politics – could make an important contribution to the Adult Education Department of the Ontario Institute for Studies in Education (O.I.S.E.), where he was chair. As mentor, adversary, and friend, Roby had an enormous influence on me. At O.I.S.E. I went through a protracted M.A. and then a protracted Ed.D. – making up altogether more than twenty years of contact with its Adult Education Department. Through this link I have been exposed to some of the academic writing in critical pedagogy and feminist theory. As an extension of these interests, I have been involved with the International Council for Adult Education, and more recently the Canadian Association for Adult Education. These networks have provided me with a certain balance against the rhythms and concerns of union education.

Third, there is my continuing participation in the politics of southern Ontario, focusing especially on helping to build the small-scale community organizations that sustain critical social movements. By conducting workshops with school principals, trustees, parents, or students, I have engaged in the debates around formal education in my community. In the Mayworks Festival of Working People and the Arts and the Ontario Workers Arts and Heritage Centre, I have helped to create platforms through which workers and their allies can express our creative visions. Through the Doris Marshall Institute, I have had access to anti-racist education, community animation, and government policy-making. I have also been involved sporadically in the educational and labour-policy processes of the New Democratic Party. In this direct political activism, my issues are usually centred on democratic practice, in reaction to the top-down processes that my allies continue to tell me are only required temporarily.

The fourth part of my life, and the most difficult to sum up tidily, is family. This dimension of my life has been turbulent and powerful, to the point where for sustained periods union work has been handled on automatic pilot, with what energy I could summon. In my experience this is also true for many other brothers and sisters in unions, but they hesitate to speak of it for fear of being judged as "lacking in commitment" to the movement.

When I was first considering the Steelworker job, I asked Bert Munro whether the union would make allowances for my family responsibilities. He answered that his wife had brought up his children, but he would respect any decision I might make to handle parenting differently and he would never instruct me to take assignments at the expense of my family. Then he paused, and added, "I won't have to instruct you. The members are as brutal an employer as you will ever encounter. If you can explain to them why you need to stay home with your children, you'll have no problem with me."

Bert honoured his word, but I found that in the Steelworkers and later in the CWC my colleagues and the local union leaders would make few allowances for family time. There was little tolerance for someone who broke off work in order to parent. To share child care and other family responsibilities fairly required a "double day" of effort – a huge strain even for someone with a relatively high level of personal energy.

My fourteen-year marriage to Anita Shilton ended in 1983, five years after I started union work, and we have shared custody of our two daughters in the years since. For five years I lived with Catherine Macleod. In 1993 I became married to Barb Thomas. Each of these spirited and dynamic women has shared and influenced my union work. My relations with my daughters Danielle and Nyranne have simply been the richest source of learning and inspiration in my life.

Some critics might consider these four dimensions of my life as "baggage" and expect me to leave them at the door when entering union education. Yet I have found that the bond of solidarity with others becomes stronger as I open up this baggage. Indeed, as one who still travels a lot, I make a practice of keeping my baggage within sight as much as possible.

And I have found that other activists, when intense learning is under way, find my "baggage" and their own to be an invaluable resource.

Still, my identity as a union educator isn't at all secondary in my life. I have taken on that role and asserted it enthusiastically, even tediously according to some of my friends. Hence my doubts and proposals about the movement are the work not just of a "conscious romantic" but also of a "connected critic."

My critique, then, is not an abstract expose but rather a proposal for change in which I personally will be engaged. This bond of loyalty is captured in the classic remark by Camus: "I believe in justice, but I will defend my mother before justice."[4] It is not merely love of teaching, but love for the people with whom I have taught that continues to motivate my work. In that double sense, this study is a labour of love.

In my experience, love is a more powerful motivator than duty, whether of the political or professional sort. In the immortal doggerel of Ogden Nash:

O Duty
Why hast Thou not the visage of a sweetie or a cutie?
Why glitter Thy spectacles so ominously?
Why art Thou clad so abominously?
Why art Thou so different from Venus
And why do Thou and I have so few interests mutually in common
Between us?[5]

Indeed, the labour movement will be stronger when it works more from love and less from duty.

THREE

UNION CULTURE:
A BIRD'S EYE VIEW

∎ ∎ ∎

We need to say what many of us know in experience: ... that the struggle to learn, to describe, to understand, to educate, is a central and necessary part of our humanity.

This struggle is not begun at second hand, after reality has occurred. It is, in itself, a major way in which reality is continually formed and changed. What we call society is not only a network of political and economic arrangements, but also a process of learning and communication.

— Raymond Williams, *Communications*

When he took the seat beside me, I smelled power – traces of cologne and dry cleaning fluid drifting over to me. His suit was free of annoying wrinkles. We acknowledged each other politely, and I huddled against the airplane window, trying to steal a few more minutes of sleep.

The plane was heading to Ottawa, taking off from Terminal 2 in Toronto at seven o'clock on a dark January morning in 1984. For my fellow passenger, the airplane was clearly public space, and he was used to attention. He swept open the "Report on Business," bumping a flight attendant and waiting for her to apologize for being in his way. When our food trays were delivered, he nudged me awake in a manner suggesting he wasn't afraid of exerting a little control over seats, situations, and strangers.

"What takes you to the nation's capital?" he asked cheerily, while I tried to decide what to do with a cheese omelette that seemed decidedly petrochemical in origin.

"A union course." I made a snap decision, both about answering and taking a bite.

"You mean you work with unions?" His nose crinkled as though I were panhandling in a chic restaurant. Unusually, he didn't dive back into his stock quotations to escape. Instead he started to talk, and I guessed he must be in sales, a compulsive conversationalist.

By then I had become aware of just how out of place I was as a unionist on that particular flight. Apparently your average workers – or their representatives – don't belong on early morning shuttle flights. It was too early for children or old people, and few women could be seen down the rows of suits. Calculators were out next to the breakfast trays, as slim, white, middle-aged men prepared for their important meetings with government and business ... men who had pulled themselves out of bed before dawn to secure their daily place on the corporate ladder. The early morning flights are occupied by middle-level managers with thick briefcases. Their superiors travel on mid-morning flights with slimmer briefcases.

As I started into a conversation, I remembered some fatherly advice I had got when I first joined the Steelworkers. It came from Bert Munro, the Assistant to the National Director. One time, leaning across a salad bar in an Orillia chain restaurant, Bert told me to conserve energy by limiting my time with the establishment movers and shakers. "If you fly too much with the ducks, you'll start to quack."

But it was too late now. This suit was subtly talking about the interplay among leaders in business and government. His heart seemed to be in the right place on broad social issues – on medicare, day care, and pensions we reached some friendly agreement. But it was another story when we got to "big unions." He saw unions as social bullies, bringing native cunning or brute force to bear on weak spots in the system for their own narrow benefit.

By now several voices were awake inside me, arguing amongst themselves with increasing heat. I pulled my electric shaver out of the briefcase and escaped to the washroom. There, looking in the mirror, I thought about how I would like to buckle him, and all of his corporate cronies, into their seats and then take over the plane's intercom. While circling Ottawa, I would rant at them, in both official languages. I would tell the stories of communities that have experienced corporate betrayal, list broken promises made by company managers, talk about the pain and humiliation felt by decent people living through economic depression while the media trumpet "recovery." I would force them to pledge that only people who have dinner with an unemployed person at least once a month would be allowed to talk about economics.

I returned to my seat as the familiar bilingual Canadian announcement came telling us that we were "commencing our descent towards Ottawa." I could imagine members of my union far down below the clouds scraping ice off windshields, breathing into their gloves for warmth, stomping snow off boots and coaxing cars out of driveways onto roads. I'd be meeting with them within the hour, and my feet would be firmly back on the ground in more ways than one.

I talked about this experience in that day's course, and others shared similar clashes and fantasies. Unions are not simple structures. They are not simple collections of people. Their inner workings are as complex and subtle as those of the employers they face. The assumption that working-class institutions are one-dimensional and easily definable is anchored in a deeply false stereotype of working people.

Active unionists like myself tend to have a double reaction when we are faced with unexamined prejudices about our organizations. These also come up in what I call the "barbecue chats," the occasions when neighbours, relatives, and co-workers challenge union activists about why we are "wasting our time" in organizations that they assume to be outmoded, corrupt, inequitable, strike-happy, bureaucratized, unproductive – you name it. On such occasions we usually respond with information that challenges the stereotypes. We remind our friends that labour has long been the social conscience of this country. Not so long ago, wages were at poverty levels, hours of work were long, and non-wage benefits such as pensions, holidays, and sick leave were not widely available. In democratizing social values and initiating the welfare state, the union movement has had a dramatically positive impact on the quality of life for all Canadians. Along with bilingualism and medicare, strong unions are a key element in the Canadian sense of difference from Americans, which is why all three are under attack by the right in efforts to "harmonize" Canada's political economy with that of the United States.

Union culture is the web of knowledge and prejudice, common sense, good sense, and nonsense that union activists share. It is the way things are done among unionists. It constitutes the social glue of the movement and distinguishes union activists from other people. It may not be perfect, but it is ours. Particularly it is ours when compared to the version put forth by marketers of "corporate cultures," in which workers and their unions are supposed to become junior partners.

A sweeping concept like "union culture" needs to be used cautiously. It is a bit like using the term "workers" in a blanket way that masks gender, race, and other identities – including geographical location – that shape people's experience, sometimes more profoundly. In the future we may have to talk of "union cultures" in the same way that many people now speak of "feminisms."[1]

The idea of union culture has been useful for me in two locations: in building unions internally and in defending them externally. In my introductory courses for union activists, the concept has helped to situate the personal changes they experienced and the bonds they spontaneously found with unionists from other workplaces. In government and academic conferences, in discussions of labour-market and worker education issues, the term has reinforced the legitimacy of the labour speakers.

There are ten dynamics, ten cross-currents, that I use to locate my work in the union movement. Each of these pairs represents a relationship, a creative tension, and I think they help us identify personal experiences and supports and barriers in the movement. We'll take a look at them one by one.

(1) Diverse/cohesive

Canada's unionists are not a homogeneous lot. The range of social and organizational identities in Canada's labour movement is in one sense an index of health – the fruit of efforts to organize across the many variations within working-class culture. For union leaders at all levels, that range is also a continuing challenge: to develop a solidarity that is negotiated rather than assumed. While unions are diverse, the union activist is continually searching for common ground, guided by the adage that "in unity is strength."

For me, a good example of these differences came in the work of Alex Dagg, a union educator who worked next door to me in the late 1980s. Her office was in the Labour Lyceum, which for many years housed the offices of textile and garment industry unions. Most of the members of her union, the International Ladies Garment Workers, were immigrant women, and she spent much of her time arranging courses in English as a Second Language. In my union's telecommunications sector nearly all the members had a high school diploma, and fluency in English was taken for granted. Her budget was minimal, because the globalization of garment manufacturing had leached away the dues income of the union, while

Photograph exhibited at the Mayworks Festival in 1992.

mine was relatively steady. Her political priorities had to do with free trade and homework, while ours were with deregulation and workplace reorganization. Both of us were union educators, but the social identities that we dealt with were entirely different.[2]

But, while it is diverse, the union movement is not necessarily scattered. According to historian Bryan Palmer's description of Canadian working-class culture:

> This was, for long periods of our history, an inert culture. For all of the cultural inertia of the working class, however, its apparent fragmentation, acquiescence, and accommodation could change with the drop of a hat or, more precisely, the drop of a wage, the demise of a skill, or the restructuring of a job.[3]

The labour movement's reflex towards unity is based on the deep understanding that "united we stand, divided we fall." The cohesion of the union movement is about groups, not about individuals. It is based on the practical knowledge that management listens to an organized group of workers completely differently than it would listen to an individual rebel.

In most of North America, so deeply imbued with individualism, building this cohesion means swimming against the cultural stream.[4] One of the keys to the strength of Quebec's labour movement, for instance, is precisely the sense of collective identity, shared heritage, in that nation as a whole. The collectivity that undergirds the union culture can be sustained and expanded, I believe, but not without a sweeping change in the broader culture.

Today, as more women and people of colour raise their voices within the movement, leadership requires knitting together a coalition of interests rather than articulating a pre-existing consensus. Still, the reflex of cohesion helps balance the momentum towards fragmentation.

(2) Oppressive/affirmative

There is difference within the labour movement, and there are also hierarchies. While union policies may assert the need for equity in matters of gender, race, and other forms of difference, a daily struggle takes place across all of these dimensions of union life. Inevitably, an educator in the union culture plays a role, for better or for worse, in some manifestation of systemic oppression.

In my courses I am sharply challenged by women whenever I am lazy or careless enough to assume that my experience represents some kind of norm. I have to consciously resist working from a shallow image of union solidarity that excludes others, leaving them out because their social identities differ from mine. In their study of women's role in unions, Linda Briskin and Patricia McDermott point out:

> Closely related to the theme of making gender visible is the need to challenge the tendency to use the male as 'the standard'. This tendency takes two pernicious forms: first, the assumption that the experience of men is generic to both women and men, an assumption which makes the significance of gender completely invisible; and second, the assumption that men's reality should establish 'the norm' against which women are measured, thereby implying that women are atypical and should change to conform to the male model.[5]

A vivid reminder of the strength of these forces, and of my own limited skill and power in addressing them, came in a member's living room in 1981. In Elkford, B.C., where I was doing a three-day Facing Management course, I met Ezekiel Ugoalah and his wife Augusta, who had come six years earlier from Nigeria. Zeke was a member of the Steelworkers local at the Fording Coal company, which had gone on strike two months before my visit, mostly over the issue of safety hazards in the mine.

Zeke was the only black person in the course and he had held his space as we drew out social patterns – of young and old, of men and women, of native-born and immigrant, of employed and unemployed. Despite the obvious need for solidarity in a strike, I thought we needed to acknowledge these differences. What we didn't need was to create a false front that would be incapable of weathering the storm of a strike.

At the end of the course Zeke invited me back to his house. The living room walls were covered with certificates. They came from high school graduation and welding courses, and included his wife Augusta's university degree. But one small label in another place caught my eye: a piece of masking tape starting to peel off the base of the table lamp, with a price of $20 marked on it in ballpoint pen.

Zeke and Augusta were selling the contents of their house, part of the stake they had built in six years of hard work. They were getting ready to move to a larger urban centre. They had already mailed a downpayment on a new house to London, Ontario, and the university there had accepted Augusta's transcripts. Zeke and Augusta were solid union supporters – they hadn't flinched since the strike vote – but underneath was the sense that their hopes were being ground up in a conflict not of their own making.

Zeke and Augusta were leaving of their own free choice, but at the same time no one in the union was reaching out to keep them involved, and the union offered no broad-based structure in which they could continue to have a role once Zeke's employment ended. While they were intensely pro-union, they had to face the reality that Canada's labour movement was still dominated by men – Canadian-born men, white men with long service to a single employer. They couldn't easily fit in.[6]

Whether it is a matter of race, gender, educational level, or some other aspect of social identity, many active members are at a disadvantage in union structures. Unions can either reinforce or challenge these systemic inequities. Women, for example, are a significant presence in local union leadership, but are less than proportionally represented in union staff.[7] Still, action has occurred in three important ways: internally, in collective bargaining, and in public education. Unions' membership education programs address equity issues, and the structures have been adapted to include designated positions for groups traditionally excluded. Bargaining proposals frequently include pay equity and other ways of addressing problems of past and systemic discrimination. Participation in a range of public coalitions on issues from child care to employment equity has

33

Workers of different cultural and racial backgrounds are sometimes pitted against one another, as in the Postal Workers strike of 1992.

carried union leaders and union resources into the broader struggles against racism and sexism.

Treatment of the issue of sexual harassment provides an indicator of the progress made since the late 1970s when the Steelworkers' functions would tolerate behaviour that insulted women. In the 1990s most unions have explicit policy statements on sexual, racial, and personal harassment. At union events representatives are often designated to handle any such incidents that might occur. While problems remain, the boundaries of the culture have shifted greatly during these years to become more inclusive, more welcoming. Most importantly, perhaps, unions have become more aware of difference *as a resource* rather than a threat.

(3) Passionate/bureaucratized

My daughter Danielle had made the trip to the course in Elkford with me, and when we returned her strongest impression was that strikes meant adults had time to spend with their children.[8] In Elkford we had seen workers who were fully committed to their community as well as to the strike. People were running bulk food distribution, clearing the ski hill, renovating the union hall, and organizing events with their children that didn't cost money. They were using their time, waiting for the company to move their way. As happens more often than not in a strike situation, the union adrenalin was flowing.

The experience of collective passion is common in union life. Yet unions also have a capacity for mind-numbing detail. Even in a strike like the one in Elkford the system of weekly strike pay relies on a worker doing full picket duty, which creates a huge record-keeping job. Apart from the strike situation, in the regular course of activities a local has to meticulously check claims for lost time and expenses. In turn the grievance system generates mounds of paper, often focused on interpretation of a single word or brief phrase.

This administration is necessary and important. It is central not just to a union's day-to-day work but also to monitoring the integrity of union leadership and the effectiveness of union representation. Yet it chills the climate of the movement, and for those who are hooked on protocols and routines, who continually calculate odds rather than leading with the heart, it provides their preferred weapons for internal battles.[9]

Leaders who are personally secure and organizationally skilled – who can skilfully balance passion and bureaucracy – are rare in any milieu. One such person is Fred Pomeroy, founding president of the CWC and later treasurer and then president of the CEP. One afternoon in early 1990 Fred and I had a lengthy debate about union strategy in a Regina coffee shop. After a couple of hours I deferred to his position, mainly because I found myself overwhelmed by all the information he had at his fingertips. A few days later Fred sent me a memo reminding me not to back down in private arguments with him: "I'm elected, so I'll have to make the decision, but the staff close to me have to hold their ground. I need your views, not your agreement to my views."

To stand your ground as a union activist, then, requires keeping an open heart and precisely accurate accounts. And it requires some luck to have influential leaders nearby who welcome change and challenge rather than trying to squash it.

(4) Informal / accountable

The most visible and easily recorded aspects of union life are not always the most significant. Union policy statements, even course outlines, can be pulled from files, but it is harder to trace the informal conversations and networks that they originated in. Attention to these informal occasions is as essential as professional rigour in union assignments. Indeed, unionists tend to scrutinize behaviour outside formal sessions as carefully as they do any lecture within a course.

During cutback time at the Alcan plant in Kingston, Ontario, I met Jim, twenty-five years old, heavy-set, with black metallic-shiny hair that seemed to match his jeans.[10] We were taking a break from a course, getting a coffee, and Jim grinned tentatively at me before beginning to talk. He had become anxious the week before, when he heard a welding robot was being moved into the plant. After hearing from the company and from me, he felt his own job was safe; but he feared for his younger brother, who had plans of quitting high school and getting a job at Alcan. Jim wanted to know what I thought of his brother's prospects. I could only say that we were all working on educated guesses when it came to job security. My guess was that without a "trade ticket" his brother would never work more than six months at a time for Alcan.

We both took a sip of coffee, frowning almost in unison at the bitterness. Jim thanked me for telling him straight, and smiled. Then we went back into the formal session. He was a rank-and-filer, while I was on union staff, but our meeting ground was the union culture. Our basis of communication, at that point, was informal.

Nothing in that class was as clear or as important as the contact with Jim over coffee. No doubt there were other moments during that day when Jim sized me up, other moments when I didn't even realize that my work for the union was on trial. I found out later on that Jim was respected among his fellow workers and that he had afterwards spoken positively about me and the union on the floor of the plant. In the informal logic of that local union, my word was now good. I was inside the network of trust. This meant I had room to be fully myself and that I could call for a certain openness among the people I dealt with. Mistakes could be forgiven, misunderstandings straightened out . . . I was at home.

This trust must be earned again and again, because union representatives at all levels are subject to strict accountability. The leash is even shorter for elected national leaders than for appointed staff like myself. The actions of union leaders come under continuous scrutiny and public criticism. Furthermore, challengers often defeat incumbents' most carefully laid plans to remain in power.[11] While it is informal, the union culture is also one of strict accountability, both for internal educators and for elected officials.

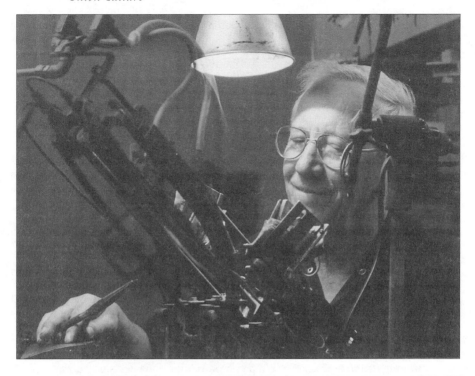

Member at work in CEP workplace.

(5) Subordinate/ adversarial

In terms of power, the labour movement in Canada plays second fiddle to management – in the making of collective agreements, in decisions affecting the work process itself, and in the wider, conventional thinking of the political economy. Rather than the overwhelmingly strong force painted in the mass media, unions are in fact quite weak. You only have to take a look at the "management rights" clause in any Canadian collective agreement to be convinced of the subordinate role of unions.[12] While employees can work through their union to challenge management power, their collective agreements explicitly accept the management right to control the work environment and the workforce. The remainder of the document, however lengthy, merely specifies the exceptions to management rule. On those points in which the contract is silent, management rights govern. This means that residual powers or unanticipated incidents revert in principle to the benefit of management.

As a result it simply does not occur to most managements to engage the union in matters other than those specifically spelled out in the agreement. With emerging issues like technological change, this can have broad and damaging results. At the Alcan plant in Kingston, for instance, the bargaining relationship, with effective managers, had been mature and positive. One day the plant manager mentioned in passing to the local union president that they were planning to bring a robot into the fabricating section. The machine would affect the jobs of forty people, but the company wasn't sure how things would work out and therefore didn't want to get into detailed discussions with the union about transfers or training or layoffs.

The local president Doug Tousignant and I had a tough time convincing that manager to put the robot in a warehouse for a month and to allow us to meet with the employees on company time to inform them about their rights in the new situation. The manager wasn't backward or hostile. He simply never imagined that the union would be upset or would have anything positive to contribute to the problems of productivity and competition that he faced. He wasn't out to bust the union, but felt quite safe in ignoring it.

In shutdowns and cutbacks this subordination leaves a bitter taste among union activists. When a company makes its decisions unilaterally, the union is left to deal with the employees' anger and sense of betrayal. When union leaders come into local union meetings, members scream at them because the leaders are the only ones who have to listen. Management can cancel at will an "open door policy," government officials can deflect calls and postpone meetings, but a local union president has no place to hide from the members, either in the workplace or in the monthly meetings where the decisions on all significant local union matters are made.

Writing of the closing of the Inglis plant in downtown Toronto, David Sobel and Susan Meurer say: "The wrecker's ball eventually destroys more than the bricks; it wipes out the mortar as well. Workers' culture is the mortar between the bricks, the material that cements workers together, and makes the hardness and roughness of daily work in a factory bearable. Such a loss is profound and irredeemable."[13]

A responsive union leader takes to heart the sorrow and anger from these losses and applies them to put energy back into union work. Some wags argue that the scrappiness of union leaders flows from a personality disorder, but in truth it comes from a sense of structural logic – it flows from the subordinate status of workers and their organizations. Over years of setbacks, the injustice of this situation builds into a slow-burning anger, which in turns leads to occasional public outbursts by union leaders. We pay a personal psychological price for the corroding force of this anger.

As long as workers and their organizations are treated with so little respect in Canada, unions won't find it safe to adopt any stance other than an adversarial one. The scepticism with which unionists greet offers of "partnership" from employers and governments must be understood in this historical context. In Canada our courts are adversarial and our elections are adversarial – which is considered a sign of justice and democracy. Labour-management relations are adversarial too, but this is considered an anachronism, a sign of outmoded attitudes.

(6) Oral/literal

Part of the reason that the wider public knows so little about unions is that so little of the internal wisdom is written down. When written text does come into play, it is treated in detail, rather than in broad conceptual terms.

The importance of this became clear to me after a meeting in Sault Ste. Marie, only a few weeks after I began working with the Steelworkers. Staff and local activists in the Algoma Steel and associated locals had made a number of suggestions for future courses in that area, and I had dutifully taken detailed notes. After getting back to the office I wrote up minutes of the meeting and forwarded them to the Sault area supervisor, Bernie Schultz.

I was completely unprepared for the phone call I got three days later from Schultz. He clearly wasn't happy. "What the hell are you doing with these minutes?" he asked.

"Oh . . . did I quote you incorrectly?"

"That's not the point, you asshole." I noted that senior staff don't mince words. "You sent copies to your director and my director," he said. "I know you're trying to get somebody – or you wouldn't have put it in writing like that. Are you trying to get me?"

"No, not at all. I'm trying to keep clear who is supposed to do what after our meeting."

"All right, you're new," Schultz said. "I'll give you another chance. But I was already clear on what I'm supposed to do. If you aren't, you can write all the notes you like. But you keep them in your own office. A memo like that is a weapon. The next one I get from you, I'll send a weapon back."

A little shell-shocked, I protested my innocence. But looking back now

I think Schultz was right. The memo was a weapon, a defensive weapon, a reflection of my fear of making mistakes. What he and the locals in his area needed to know was what I planned to do. When I decided on a course of action I should send them memos to that effect . . . short memos.

As part of my acculturation, I almost stopped writing memos. My writing style became so concise that friends outside the movement found it cryptic. Like my colleague in the Sault, I had begun to see the written word as a last resort for internal communication.[14] I came to realize the weight of history in this stance. In the early days of Canadian unions, activists communicated orally among themselves because their work was a "criminal conspiracy in restraint of trade."

For outside interaction, however, written text is central. Collective agreements and labour legislation – formal, dense, and detailed – dominate the encounter of unions with employers and governments. In reading such texts, unionists pay excruciating attention to detail, often based on experience in grievance handling, where the difference between management "may" promote the senior applicant and management "shall" promote the senior applicant can be decisive in an arbitration case. Similarly, the difference between legislation that "encourages" safe working conditions and regulations that "require" certain standards of safety can be a matter of life and death.

Not surprisingly, then, unionists have developed a methodical and literal relation to written text. On paper, union input tends to be precise and defensive; in verbal communications, off the record, unionists are more eloquent and spontaneous.

(7) *Voluntary/professional*

The drama of union life is largely played out on a stage of voluntary involvement and dedication. For example, while my own professional skills as an educator might be valued in a seminar, they are secondary to the question of whether I show up in the early morning to support a group of members in trouble. The emphasis on commitment over skill is both a strength and a weakness when it comes to representing the membership effectively.

As a strength, this emphasis multiplies the time people can commit to union work. The Steelworkers had access to over a hundred part-time local union instructors who, with some initial training and continual coaching, could meet most needs without earning extra money. Unions overcome the chronic problem of overextension through this kind of voluntary involvement. The needs of union members are huge, and their organizations are under-resourced. Full-time staff and officials are usually overwhelmed with work and all too often become addicted to the job.[15]

In this context the practice of "professionalism" represents a problem. While we now tend to recognize the intuitive and judgemental aspects of professional action, working traditions promote the objective, rational, and impersonal application of skill. This approach has left most working-class people on the losing end, time after time. Whether in the legal, educational, medical, or other fields, an "objective" approach usually works out to the benefit of the strong, and few unionists have clashed with other institutions from a position of strength. The depth of the outrage shows in the huge number of hostile jokes about lawyers among unionists. In any case, "objective" professionalism clashes directly with the passionate commitment to a cause that dominates union life. I have found that using the term "craft" rather than "profession" is consistent with the workplace culture of many of the tradespeople in my courses. It points to the fact that dedication isn't enough when you face the complex issues of the labour relations system: unions wanting to be effective need to support activists in developing special areas of skill and knowledge. It also asserts the legitimacy of contributions by radical professionals, committed craftspeople.

Nonetheless, it is often difficult to secure the conditions of work in which craft can actually be deployed. Limited budgets, large numbers of participants in courses, uncomfortable meeting rooms, and last-minute changes in schedules and locations all conspire to limit the effectiveness of union education. Yet the demand from members, and the need for elected leaders to meet this demand, combine to exert constant pressure. By voluntary effort, by dedication, union educators simply do our best, often in conditions that a strictly professional educator would reject because of the seeming impossibility of performing up to acceptable standards.

(8) Rebellious / disciplined

Shortly before Christmas 1986, phone operators in Hamilton had started getting shocks on the job. When they told the company about them, the firm called them something else, ESDs, or electro-static discharges. I guess the word shock was too scary. As a solution the company issued bracelets to the operators so they could snap a ground cord onto their wrists, thereby draining away any buildup of static electricity and, to some extent, reducing the risk of shock.[16] Operators called the bracelet and cable their "ball and chain."

In addition to their ball and chain outfits, the operators were held in position by their headsets, which they called the "umbilical cord." They were under constant pressure to reduce the time spent on each call, which on average was under twenty seconds and getting faster every year. Their work was machine-paced, isolated, and under continuous electronic surveillance. They were torn between the desire to provide good customer service and the pressure to speed up.

The stress-load on these workers, almost all women, was heavy. In the high-tech workplace, the strain of work is no longer on the back, but on the nerves. Work stress has shifted from the spine to the central nervous system.

Unionism is about rebellion against the arbitrary power of management. I handled a scheduling problem for one of these operators, Marlene, whose rebellion kept bumping into the disciplines of the slow and cumbersome grievance procedure.[17] After the automation of their work had eroded their unit to the point that they were still junior employees after eleven years of service, Marlene and a co-worker had lodged a grievance over shift scheduling. Because shifts were assigned on the basis of strict seniority, they had no control over their working schedules. Shortly after they were hired, the phone company had accelerated the substitution of technology for employees, and they could foresee a further decade of split shifts, inconvenient locations, and other irritants as senior employees exercised their contractual rights.

At one point in the procedure Marlene leaned across the table and said to a senior manager, "Do you realize I haven't had a weekday dinner at home with my husband in six weeks? We can't really talk about this properly until you have worked my shifts for six weeks." The manager harrumphed about the differences between bargaining unit employees and supervisors, but the point stood.

In the end Marlene lost the case. Yet she accepted her loss and became more involved in the union because she felt the process had been handled in a fair and supportive way. In the next round of bargaining, she made proposals for a revision of the collective agreement to address situations like her own. She understood the link between individual rebellion and collective discipline.

The impatient, rebellious streak of unionism – whether it is opposing employers or the leadership within the union movement itself – needs to be balanced by disciplined, strategic judgement of how best to secure progress on an issue over the long haul. This discipline is essential for the personal survival of union activists and of their organization. The labour movement has been built by the patient, disciplined effort of workers like Marlene who chip away at the arbitrary exercise of management power.

(9) Collective / contentious

While union life is known for its collective dynamic – its essence is bringing people together to solve problems – the key positions in the labour
movement are filled in electoral contests. Union leaders are dependent
upon membership support and must be re-elected, unlike corporation
heads. But by their very nature elections force people to make choices,
and the process of making those choices can create frictions and divisions.
This means that rivalry is structured into the labour movement.

This dynamic has an impact on union education. When a newly elected president of a local union attends a weekend union course on how to
run meetings, he or she has strong pressures for learning, apart from
intrinsic motivation. After all, in almost all cases, the local's membership
has voted funding to pay for attendance at the course. At the first meeting
after the course the local will expect the participant not only to report
back on what the course delivered but also to offer a practical demonstration of the lessons learned. If the local meeting gains a better balance of
order and participation, then all is well. If not, members will undoubtedly
raise questions about the costs of enrolment and lost wages paid by the
local, and about the materials and resource people at the class itself. And
someone will begin to start talking about running for office in order to
correct the problem or eliminate the waste.

The partisan factor in union life often surprises newcomers, and
indeed can turn them off. Yet there seems to be no way to cut off the
strands of ambition, friction, and turf battles without cutting out elections. At times this is a painful reality, because good people can be unfair-
ly defeated by manipulative and lazy people. My own courses have
become a terrain for competing factions to recruit supporters, at the
expense of real learning.

One of the personal challenges of union activism is to keep your collective vision clear while steering carefully around electoral ambushes.
Some people decide to handle union politics as a team, choosing their side
before making up their mind on the issue at hand. My preference is to
work through issues first and then try to influence all sides in the political
arena to take a particular action. Both approaches have their problems.
Yet both recognize elections as a motor for union democracy. Like the vote
to ratify or reject a tentative agreement, the vote in union elections acts as
a sharp, sometimes brutal reminder to union leaders that their power
rests on the kind of representation they provide.

Often the skirmishes are over electoral processes outside the union.
The classic debate over the partisan political involvement of unions con-

tinues during the lunch breaks of most union conferences and courses. Journalist Tom Walkom summarizes it in this remark about labour's influence within the New Democratic Party:

> At one level, the thirty-two-year-old relationship had been a flop. No matter what influence labour leaders won inside the party, the majority of the rank and file had stubbornly refused to vote NDP. And whenever NDP governments came to power – most notably in British Columbia under Dave Barrett in the 1970's and in Saskatchewan under Allan Blakeney in the 1980's – labour's interest had been sacrificed on the altar of the public good. . . . [Yet] without its own party, no matter how flawed, Canadian labour would find itself in the same position as the U.S. unions, forced to form tactical alliances with right-wing political parties over which they had no control.[18]

Certainly the relation of internal union elections and public parliamentary elections is one of the delicate political chemistries in Canadian labour. Some of my friends have chosen the parliamentary route to implement their political visions, and I have always been intrigued by and respectful about how that path works. My own focus has been in the civil society, in the web of voluntary organizations set up in the working class and the political left to challenge the power elites. And I have learned that education cannot be immune from the contentious aspect of union life, even as it works from and builds the vision of collectivity. As singer Danielle Messia puts it:

> I'm writing with the sleeping hand
> Not the one clenched in a fist
> No trained and seasoned warrior
> It lacks the power-seeker's twist
> But look, I'm now exploring
> Celebrating by my song
> Back roads, forgotten treasures,
> Paths neglected for too long.[19]

(10) Servicing/mobilizing
Every day union activists live with a tension between service and mobilization, between the need for practical help and the desire for broader social transformation. In how we structure our time, choose our reading,

direct our conversations, and chart our futures, we balance these two integral parts of union life.

The two dimensions can easily be traced in union education. Courses should be in the business of providing good technical skills and learning for the elected representatives of the membership. In this sense, education is a service. After all, the members pay the dues, and many of them look at the union as a fee-for-service arrangement. Whether they are involved in grievances, collective bargaining, safety and health programs, or education, members have a right to demand the best possible quality of service. While this may seem far from the lofty motives ascribed to the rank and file by many academic commentators on the labour movement, I think it is an entirely legitimate attitude for members. Good, consistent, quality service from an organization is hard to come by, and many workers choose to act as informed consumers when it comes to union membership.

Yet on its own this approach reinforces a kind of business unionism, a mode of working from the narrow self-interest of the members. The main problems facing workers in Canada cannot be resolved by service alone. Whether the issue is the introduction of a robot in Kingston, a strike in Elkford, or an electronic sweatshop in Hamilton, employers will only address some worker needs when a majority of union members speak and act collectively to raise their concerns. Then union education can join in to help build the enthusiasm and provide the skills needed for mobilization. In my view, social unionism works from the enlightened self-interest of the members, judging the time for service and the time for mobilization.

■ ■ ■ ■

These ten cross-currents in the union culture indicate, I hope, the intricacy and fascination of navigating along this particular stream. As an educator I have seen waves and whirlpools, and I know that the shortest distance to my goals has rarely been along a straight line. The concept of union culture has been a tool for guiding my work, for making it as effective as possible.

Shortly after joining the Communications and Electrical Workers of Canada in 1986 I wrote an education manifesto that was included in teaching manuals used in the Ontario region of the union. The statement outlined four end goals for the program:

- Dignity on the job – As union activists, we need to feel confidence in ourselves and our backup team. We have the right to accurate information about the economic, technological, and political forces that have an impact on the security and quality of our jobs.

- Democracy in the union – We equip workers to raise their voices on the job, and we do not silence them in the union. Our education program is participatory, building on the creativity and experience of the members.

- Responsibility in the society – Ours is more than a business union. It is part of the broad movement for social progress in Canada. Issues such as free trade and pay equity are an integral part of our education agenda, and so too are the skills needed to debate them in public.

- The grassroots, something to build on – Information is power. Our program aims to empower rank and file union members. By developing confidence and skills, we can defend and extend the rights of all workers.[20]

This educational statement works within the traditions of the union culture. It is also a political statement, a taking of sides within the labour movement. The program it supports will not be a "neutral" education, but will shamelessly opt for the rights of workers – and fight back against the corporate agenda. The statement offers an invitation to members, an opportunity for involvement, rather than a prescription for what they should do.

I've since found that the themes it raises – of dignity, democracy, responsibility, and grassroots action – have resonance as union values. Through successes and setbacks, always the conscious romantic, I have, along with many others, fought for these values within the richness of the union culture.

FOUR

COMING TO TERMS

∎ ∎ ∎ ∎

Where drought is the epic then there must be some
who persist, not by species-betrayal
but by changing themselves
minutely, by a constant study
of the price of continuity
a steady bargain with the way things are.
                    – Adrienne Rich, "The Desert as Garden of Paradise"

Squeezed into the back seat of a small truck going up the side of an open-pit mine, I noticed my mind beginning to wander. A mine supervisor was driving, taking myself and two other unionists on a mine tour, showing us how things worked. We were crawling up the gradual incline of a ramp that went around and around the edge of the lead and zinc mine, and I wondered how the drivers of the giant ore-hauling trucks handled the monotony of making one slow trip after another. I couldn't imagine doing a whole shift without losing concentration and putting myself, and the truck, in danger of going over the edge, down into the bottom of the mine.

The trucks hauled ore blasted out of the bottom of the Cyprus Anvil mine in Faro, Yukon Territory, taking it up to the top to be dumped and left for processing. I asked the mine manager how the drivers survived the boredom. He leaned back and answered, "We hire them for that. We look for a strong back, a weak mind, and a heavy foot."

Nobody laughed. It seemed he thought he was being one of the boys. As the rest of us looked at each other and at him, we felt a certain complicity in not challenging him on the spot. But you can't get access to a mine site without being accompanied by management, and unfortunately that means you sometimes have to just grin and bear it. Afterwards, when we were alone again, one of the unionists said, "What do you expect, D'Arcy? Isn't that what our whole course is about – how arrogant these bastards really are?"

The next morning, in the formal course Facing Management, we considered the comment and its implications. There were ten men and five women participants. Some of them were shop stewards, elected in a department by twenty or thirty workers. Others were local union officers, each of them representing hundreds of members in one of the base-metal mines of British Columbia and the Yukon. In the course they looked at their workplaces through management lenses each morning and then spent the afternoons devising union strategies for responding to management control. All of the various participants could contribute from their own experiences and develop an analysis of their own situations. They compared notes on different levels of management, seeing how apparently contradictory behaviours reinforced one another as parts of an overall corporate culture.

At the time, most other union courses were based on the positions held by members; they were aimed at stewards, local officers, health and safety committee members, for example. This way it was easy for a local union to make educational decisions – if the local had three new stewards, they should be sent to the basic steward course. Courses that centred on a theme, such as political action or women's rights, were usually aimed at the most experienced local activists. Often members were sent into them with the expectation that they would run an election campaign or start a women's committee, some specific assignment to apply what they knew. The Facing Management course, to the contrary, offered learning that any worker representative would find of practical use.

As we talked, a whole layer of resentment and resistance came into focus for me. The way the cultural cards are stacked in North America, a mining engineer in his mid-thirties not only earns more than a member in the bargaining unit, but also carries certain "badges" of ability – certificates, career prospects, and social mobility – that working-class people regard with a mix of resentment and envy. When supervisors flaunt these badges in a display of class arrogance, they can unwittingly create a crack in the normal pattern by which workers are convinced that their subordination is legitimate. If carefully approached, such cracks in consent can be widened to allow for the emergence of new perceptions and possible actions.[1] Established patterns of domination can be suspended, creating an opportunity for building critical consciousness.

The course opened such cracks by critical review of management training materials on motivating employees, weakening unions, technological change, and job enrichment schemes. We discussed Taylorism and Maslow's hierarchy of needs. We talked about local conditions in Faro. Here as elsewhere in the North, there was a radical difference in housing and living conditions between Native and white residents, and at the time almost no Native people worked in the Cyprus Anvil mine. The course was in effect taking place in a cultural enclave, predominantly of workers who had moved out from Newfoundland in search of work. Classes ran for eight hours a day with evening film screenings, over five full days.

That particular morning participants told story after story about "getting back" at abusive supervisors. I repeated one of my favourites, about an incident in the late 1970s at Algoma Steel in Sault Ste. Marie. A new foreman had been throwing his weight around until one morning a mysterious series of breakdowns on the line took place. Smooth functioning only returned when a plant manager quietly assured the workers that the foreman would be transferred out at the end of the week. No formal meeting occurred, everyone saved face, and by the following Monday the problem had been solved.

One evening during the course we got together for a special dinner in the union hall with another class and workers from the mine. Like most of the buildings in northern mining towns, that one was prefabricated and had a temporary feel, much like the portable school classrooms set in place in southern Canada to take in the children of the baby boom. The hall was warmly decorated, the food abundant, and the speech by the town's mayor was warm, funny, and brief. He talked mostly about food, partly because he was the head cook for the mining camp and partly because of the power of food. A couple of years before that particular course, a nearby mine had been shut down by a wildcat strike in which the main issue was food. Complaints about cuisine in these workplaces are legion, although most outsiders, like myself, consider the quality and abundance to be remarkable. In time I came to understand that food was one point of possible resistance within a highly controlled lifestyle. The employers assigned housing, hired and fired teachers in the local school, designed recreation facilities, all without being openly challenged, but it was acceptable to complain about how the employers set menus. As with all monopoly service situations, the workers became enormously frustrated by small details that revealed indifference and arrogance.

After dinner it was time to play. Three subgroups had accepted the challenge of "doing a turn." The first skit consisted of three union members sitting on paint cans, dressed in overalls, while two "managers" in suits lectured them on the importance of raising productivity. In this and the two following skits the lines were familiar, but the slapstick was lively. The audience of about fifty provided plenty of applause. Afterwards the local's financial secretary played guitar and sang a few melancholy Newfoundland ballads. Then one participant announced a surprise closing performance. Two "co-workers" from the first skit strode in with four others behind them, all of them wearing matching union jackets and carrying matching union briefcases. The two "managers" were abruptly called up for a follow-up meeting with a union committee presenting a typed agenda and sheaf after sheaf of proposals for improving the working environment. As the managers shrugged with mock dismay at this turning of tables, everyone cheered raucously. The formal banquet was over, and the course participants got down to some serious drinking.[2]

The Facing Management course was clearly a hit in the Yukon, as it was in other places. It tapped into a need throughout the union movement to respond strategically to new management approaches. In the initial phase of developing the course, Rick Williams of Halifax was my guide and co-teacher. As the interest became too widespread for me to meet it personally, Rita Kwok Hoi Yee worked with me to develop a course leader manual, and also contributed readings, such as excerpts from the writings of Chinese philosopher Sun Tzu, which became a useful and popular part of the program.[3] In sessions like this one in the Western Canadian region of the Steelworkers, District 3, I co-taught with education representative Don Posnick, a pragmatic, witty, and dedicated colleague whose support of the course was a key to its success in the Steelworkers and elsewhere in the early 1980s. It became a fixture on the "menu" of courses offered to local unions, along with grievance handling, collective bargaining, and safety and health.

By 1984, fully 65 out of a total of 110 participants in the Steelworker summer school for western Canada were enroling by preference in the Facing Management course. With the delayering of corporations throughout the 1980s, union activists began increasingly to meet directly with

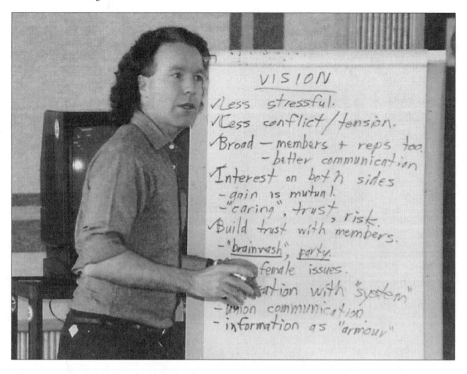

The author, teaching the Facing Management material to a group of local union officers in early 1993.

senior managers, generating a new set of learning needs for union educators to address ... and a new set of stories for Facing Management courses.

BORN IN THE SUDBURY STRIKE

The resonance of the stories told in the Facing Management courses was far beyond anything I had anticipated when the idea first germinated in my "initiation time." A request for some information had come in from Local 6500, the miners at Inco whose bitter strike in 1978–79 had shaken the Sudbury Basin socially as well as economically. After the strike employees had returned to their work sites, scattered widely throughout the area.[4] Yet during the first week or two afterwards, as they came into the union hall to swap stories about the start-up, the workers started to find some common patterns. Their supervisors were engaging in personal

I made $12 an hour at the steel mill until I was laid off.

On unemployment.

conversation – enquiring about their families, expressing concern about their financial situation, commenting on community events and sports that might form a bridge between them. It appeared that the front-line supervision at Inco was using psychology in a strategic way.

The stewards and local officers were uncertain about how to respond. They knew that during the strike the company had conducted lengthy training courses with supervisors, since the people who were kept on salary had not been able to engage in direct production and needed something constructive to do. I was asked to get my hands on some of the materials that had been used to train the managers, so that our people would know what they were dealing with. Our most provocative find was a manual that fell off a manager's desk at Michelin Tire in Nova Scotia when the company was fighting to keep the unions out. The binder, *Union Free Management and How to Keep It Free*, was a detailed training guide for supervisors and foremen, explaining how to keep employees divided.[5]

Gradually we adapted our own study guides and role-play activities to a new course design, turning the normal pattern of workplace psychology and sociology on its head. After all, substantial academic resources go into studying worker behaviour and into sharing the results of those studies with managers. The curriculum for "labour relations" is well established at universities and business schools, but "management relations" is almost unheard of, with no great wealth of research and readings it can draw on. Our work turned the searchlight the other way, exploring highlights and shadows within the management mindset.

So, I took computer classes and now I earn $6 an hour.

One recurring story in courses centred around relatively subtle efforts by supervisors to isolate a newly elected steward from fellow workers. A supervisor would enter a lunch room and pull the steward aside for a short conversation. The content might be completely frivolous – perhaps sharing a joke or commenting on workplace gossip.

After the workers returned to the job, the supervisor would discipline one of them. When the steward tried to intervene, the supervisor's body language would imply that the matter had been discussed privately with the steward ahead of time. Whatever the outcome, a seed of doubt would be planted: that the relationship between the steward and the supervisor was stronger than that between steward and member.

In our course discussion a lesson would be drawn from this: a new steward talking with management should make sure to be accompanied by at least one other worker, no matter how irrelevant the conversation may seem to be. Yet this simple guideline, known to every experienced steward and local union officer, was not evident to me at all in the early days of the course. Shared stories like this were the anchor of each course, keeping Rick Williams and I on track lest we become too absorbed in the intricacies of books saying what managers ought to be doing.

At times, street smarts and book smarts would merge. This could happen, for instance, in an activity I came to call the "politics of furniture," in which each of us would share experiences about times when the layout of a meeting room had put us at an advantage or disadvantage. This would lead into a discussion of the various ways of drawing managers out from behind their desks – that psychological shield and status symbol – to face union representatives directly. In this case handing out reference material on non-verbal communication can help equip participants with some necessary reinforcement and precise labels for their own understandings.

From this very practical, skill-building component, the course has gone on to tackle broader strategic issues. Its title alone implies a labour agenda for any and all encounters with employers. While unionists have always known that "in unity is strength," such unity cannot successfully be imposed from above except in extreme situations like strikes. Members will support their union when they feel that their union supports them. Although negotiating such a conditional relationship can be frustrating, it remains the central challenge of leadership in voluntary social movements. Repeatedly in this course, I find myself emphasizing that we capture management's attention not through personal charm and knowledge, but with effective representation and "union judo" – the art of using your opponents' weight and inertia to bring them down to your own level.

At some point in the course another key question emerges: why does management have so many allies, while unions have so few? This is, in other words, the question of relative social power and how to change it, and it opens up the debate of business unionism vs. social unionism. A business unionist will try to contain the discussion at the workplace level, arguing that issues like medicare or free trade are irrelevant. Other participants will talk about how gains at the bargaining table can be wiped out by the stroke of a politician's pen. Understandably, this kind of debate often tempts course leaders into arguing with participants. My own preference is to make my views known early and briefly and then to help the discussion along with as little intrusion as possible. By respecting the participants' starting points, and encouraging radical, critical reflection on them, I think the course leader accomplishes more than by lecturing and arguing.[6]

At times I was tempted to let a course discussion degenerate into a hate session on managers. The closest I ever came was in the dealings of the Steelworkers local in Elkford, British Columbia, with Tom Davies. Tom, a Steelworkers staff representative, had worked with the union local in the previous round of bargaining. Shortly after that process was finished he resigned and was hired by Fording Coal to deal with the union. During the next round of bargaining he used inside knowledge against his former friends, and during the strike he went on the radio to criticize the union's demands. The sense of betrayal in the local was so strong that some rage had to be vented in our course, and the unionists decided that they had to find ways of discrediting him publicly and especially of limiting his damage. But the case also made clear that as union activists (and educators) we have to draw a fine line: there is a difference between righteous anger and hatred. Anger is loaded with information and energy, while hatred contributes neither.[7] We need to focus not just on management, but also on ourselves, and we will build our own strengths more effectively through compassion and firmness than bitterness.

In any case, a course on Hating Management would not serve unionists who have to work with management every day to solve problems and negotiate settlements to disputes. The reality of a long-term human relationship often softens how workers come to see their bosses. One body of learners who kept me in line in British Columbia was the firefighters who enroled every year in my session of the course. Access to senior jobs in fire departments is almost exclusively by promotion through the ranks, and many of the leaders of the International Association of Fire Fighters (IAFF) saw themselves as potential fire chiefs. Their union sent them to the course so that they would better understand their future role as managers. These confident and conciliatory participants brought a different tone to sessions than did some of the more angry delegates from other unions, and I felt humbled at times by their matter-of-fact assessment of mutual need between managers and employees. A session that focused only on attacking managers would have alienated those learners – even worse, it would have puzzled them.

During this period political pressures on me were intensifying. As the "back to the locals" program took root throughout the Steelworkers, and the Facing Management course raised the profile of education across the movement, the tests became more frequent and more personally disturbing.

GENDER POLITICS

As my education work began to emerge from initiation time, powerful tensions of home and work commitment converged. During the early 1980s my marriage was coming apart, largely because my absorption in union work left little or no room for a good balance of home responsibilities, and little time to nurture my personal life. When issues of gender began to become more heated in the union, they escalated rapidly for me because they echoed tensions at home.

For me, the switch from the Steelworkers' masculinist work world to a feminist home and social world was tangible. On the drive home from the union office to the day care to pick up my daughters my reflexes and language patterns would shift. Outside work, with many feminist activists among our friends, I heard less about golf and football and more about abortion clinics and lesbian relationships.

Around that time the gender politics of the labour movement was changing as well. Policy papers on women's rights, women's caucuses within unions, and the "Women of Steel" initiative in my own union shifted the balance. When Deirdre Gallagher moved into the Steelworkers' National Office as communications rep, I found a colleague who pushed as well as supported me in bringing women's rights issues into the union.

This work had begun for me with the 1979 Radio Shack strike, which brought a group of women up against a transnational union-bashing employer. It continued through the union-backed production of *Moving Mountains* (1981–82), a film about women in the mining industry directed by Laura Sky. Feminist musician Arlene Mantle brought her militant songs to the week-long courses of the Steelworkers throughout the early 1980s, and we began to develop and teach women's rights courses. In those years the labour movement also addressed the issue of women's representation in its leadership positions, resulting in the decision to reserve vice-presidents' seats for women on the executives of many central labour bodies and culminating in the mid-1980s election of Shirley Carr as president of the Canadian Labour Congress.

The issue of women's role in union activity and structure – and of how much attention we should pay to women's issues in general – polarized the Steelworkers, and I was frequently caught in the middle. I made women's rights a major priority of the education program, yet during this period women made up only 15 per cent of the Steelworkers' Canadian membership. Male colleagues would protest that the changes were too rapid, and women would say the changes were coming too slowly. In Canada women were being harassed on the job, assaulted in the streets, battered at home, objectified and humiliated in the media.

My privileges as a man, and as a person of influence in the union, were up for challenge. I could explicitly bargain with women Steelworkers for mutual political support, but when we breezily assumed common interests it seemed that one of us would get surprised and hurt.

A few years later I was able to work more resiliently with this tension. I remember a high school assembly where I had been asked to speak about tech change and the future of work. Trying to break the static pattern of such compulsory occasions, I began listing some of the areas of union work that I thought students would appreciate, such as pay equity for women. A hush fell over the hall. Misinterpreting the silence, I sailed on, with the rhetorical question: "Do you know that for every dollar a man earns, a woman earns only sixty-two cents?" I paused to let the point sink in and was rocked by a roar of approval from three hundred young men.

I returned to the fray: "Last month, for the first time in my life, my spouse began earning more than me. And if you guys think that's a loss for men, you should think again . . . for me, it's a terrific deal." Now there was a roar of approval from three hundred young women.

The waves of energy in that hall reminded me of the gulf between men and women of my generation in the early 1980s. Perhaps more of this bluntness in gender politics, and more gusto in conflict, would have improved my union work. Yet that required more inner peace and strategic clarity than I could muster at the time. Often I felt isolated, ambivalent, and brittle – all of this far from being an ideal stance for promoting progressive debate in a union course.

CREATIVE SPARKS AND CONSCIOUS ROMANTICS

The theatre was a room in a fading spa hotel in Harrison, B.C. The audience was three hundred trade unionists, men and women – workers drawn together by the Canadian Labour Congress in January 1981 to a week-long course on teaching methods and trade unionism. They came from public-service offices and private-sector plants, from banks and airports, from towns and cities throughout British Columbia.

The room, called "Caesar's Forum," came complete with green walls lined with white plaster imitations of Roman statues – a place that spelled "atmosphere" to some and kitsch to most. We had used this room, the largest space available in the hotel, for our union courses all day, and during the supper break a stage had been erected. Now the lights were low, and a few broken-down chairs on the stage suggested the barroom of a hotel. A character on stage offered up the chant of a chokerman on a weekend spree in Vancouver:

> In the Grand Hotel, when the loggers come in,
> It's amusing to see the proprietor grin.
> He knows they've got money and he'll soon have it all;
> 'Come on boys, have a drink' you will hear Tommy call.[8]

In Caesar's Forum the trade unionists sat silent and attentive. This was the logger's life, larger than life, captured in a play called *Highball!* The play's effectiveness depended on its accuracy in language.

> Then the logger sat and he thought a bit,
> And he said: But it's no surprise
> What preys on my mind all of the time –
> One glance from a woman's eyes.

The tackiness of the room had receded in the face of the art on stage – and the all-too-real sense of loneliness of the logging camp, the depiction of harsh working conditions. "Highball" means top production with no regard for safety or maintenance:

> She was patched together
> 'Bout nineteen three
> By Henry Ford after a
> Three-day drinking spree;
> The heels are square
> And the axles roam free
> And he went and left the springs out
> Entirely.

When the play was over, the audience stood and cheered.

In its most effective moments, union education has generated creative sparks by involving workers both as creators and as the audience for creators. This participation as performers and observers represents more than a change of pace; it is a seed for democratizing culture. To respect, refine, and strengthen arts expression in the working class is to challenge the stereotype that unionists are by nature insensitive or uncreative. It is also to equip union activists for effectiveness in a media-saturated society. That week-long course served up by the Canadian Labour Congress in Harrison, B.C., gave a taste of the potential of mixing together unions and art.

ARTS IN UNION EDUCATION

The morning after the play in Harrison we started day three of the five-day course on teaching methods. It was clear that the performance had affected us all, especially a logger named Gary.[9] Gary was in his mid-twenties, quiet and earnest. He seemed vulnerable, and as the course leader I found myself trying to keep track of what went on to make sure he didn't get hurt. That morning Gary was second in line for practice teaching and had chosen the topic "Working Safe in the Woods." We were doing a role-play, and a group of us were pretending to be newly hired loggers.

After introducing his topic Gary called for questions, and a public service union staff representative was the first to speak up. She had breezed through her practice teaching the previous afternoon. Poised and articulate, she had already twice blown Gary out of the water in discussions on sexism in the labour movement. This time her tone was respectful, her question straightforward. She asked: "Could you tell me what a choker-man actually does?"

When Gary realized there was no hook hidden in her question, the tension gradually drained from his face. He started sketching on a flip chart, showing how the chokerman wraps a chain around the trunk of a felled tree, so that it can be dragged down a mountain slope and collected for shipment.

Then he harkened back to one of the stories in the play, a glimpse of the individual rebellions that every unionist knows:

Da cook, he cook two ways – good for da brains, pig slop for the men. So Pete, he have enough, and he yump on da table, walk up to da head, step over to da brains' table and kick all their dishes one by one crash on da floor. Da men sit and don't do nothing. A few days later, Rough House (Pete) is laid off, but da food get better right now.

This practice round of teaching was supposed to take just five minutes, enough to break the ice, but Gary was picking up momentum. He used movement and gesture to emphasize his points. His notes on the flip chart were neither abbreviated nor cluttered. His interaction with the class was lively, a delicate balance of participation with control – the classic tension of democratic educational leadership. In all of this he was demonstrating the aspects of the craft we had been working on in the course. He was eloquent, and we were all spellbound.

After thirty-five minutes Gary glanced at his watch and started to apologize to me for going over his five-minute limit. The public service staff rep was the first on her feet, and then we all stood up to applaud him. He grinned shyly, obviously both a little surprised and very pleased about what he had achieved. That moment, the highlight of the week, would not have happened without the play. The performance had touched a chord within Gary, a sense that he wasn't a loser, wasn't alone. It had made the others think twice about their stereotypes of loggers.

Arts presentations like this have brought out the creative spark in union courses. They require that educational planners provide the budget and facilities to bring in outside artists. The spark can be sustained when classroom activities like role-plays give scope to the performing streak in participants. The climate of the formal study can also allow for informal music, visual arts, and literature. That's how they did it in the remarkable learning community we called the Workers' Republic of Harrison during the early 1980s.

One evening of each course was committed to a professional arts performance of some sort, usually poetry readings or a play. The theme

Mary Rowles, union staff rep, reading from her poem "The War on Paper" at the Mayworks Festival.

always addressed workers and their unions, and the form was challenging. A second evening was committed to the other end of the arts-labour bridge. Workers need to be engaged directly in creative expression, not just mobilized as an audience for the arts. At most CLC residential courses, classes compete in writing and performing a song, creating instant "class choirs" that usually address a current political theme in a slapstick style.

A letter from a Steelworkers member, a maintenance worker in a steam generator, to an officer of his local union captures the psychological significance of this kind of worker participation in the arts. The worker was explaining why the rights that the labour movement had won on paper (in this case the right to refuse unsafe work) are so hard for most working people to exercise effectively:

From the time a man is born, the basic item of control on his behaviour is intimidation. First, the enormous difference in physical size between he and his parents. Second, the hundreds of injunctions in the form of "don't talk back." Then he encounters the institutional authority of teachers where the rule is, "Raise your hand and wait to be recognized."

By the time he reaches the workplace, it's a miracle if he speaks at all. The law may entitle a man to refuse an unsafe task, but whether he can find the courage to resist the subtleties of authority, to which he has been made subject from birth, is another matter.

Changing the law does not immediately negate 1,000 years of cultural evolution.

Arts work in the labour movement challenges these "subtleties of authority." Ideally, people whose workplaces foster passivity can find in their unions a level of emotional engagement and intellectual challenge that develops their full capacities. Another level of excitement occurs when they find themselves acting as creators in a union sing-song, or as an engaged audience for a professional production that somehow captures a sense of their own lives, both personal and in the workplace. The encounter of arts-positive unionists with union-positive artists has enriched union education with information, insights, confidence, and skill that a more inward-turned and cautious didactic approach could not have achieved.

THE VAGARIES OF UNION JOB SECURITY

While these healthy, vital activities were going on, a further current was feeding into what increasingly felt like a whirlpool, and that was my insecure status as an employee. For eighteen months in a row during 1981–82, the collapse of the U.S. steel industry was like a rock dragging down the union's membership figures. With the income from membership dues declining, expenses had to be reduced and staff had to be laid off. The experience would take its toll on the confidence of activists and the openness of the leadership.

The Steelworkers' Staff Representatives Union had insisted that the union leadership give adequate notice of layoffs and use seniority as the guiding principle. From the 1940s to the 1970s, a job with the Steelworkers union had been a job for life. While individuals had been fired or quit, since the founding of the union no staff person had ever been laid off.

Although length of service is an arbitrary measure of value to the membership, I think that in this new situation the strict seniority approach served people well. The union made no exceptions based on subjective criteria like "merit," "skill," or "essential work," measures open to manipulation. By applying this visible, public, and familiar principle, the union made sure that relations between colleagues were not damaged by the fact that some were kept on staff over others.[10]

In the end I was one of the last two people retained, the other one being a representative in Indiana I had never met, who had started work on the same date. Everyone else in North America who was hired thirteen days later than us, after March 14, 1978, was laid off, including my assistant Ian Kirkpatrick. The process was clean, objective, and painful.

Among staff the shock of the layoff created a climate of insecurity, a fear of the future that worked against the kind of participatory and problem-posing education that had been gathering momentum. We were living what the members were living. While I kept my job, I found myself

61

unable to make commitments to educational projects when I had no assurance that I would be able to carry them through.

The tension between senior and junior staff erupted at a staff meeting called to discuss the situation. Junior staff asked why layoffs were not separated between the United States, which had huge membership losses, and Canada, where the decline had been far less. Senior staff said such questions were disloyal, arguing for the advantages of the international connection. Junior staff commented that the main immediate benefit of the U.S. link was that staff pensions were paid in U.S. dollars, which was scarcely a matter of interest to the younger people who were being laid off, but, it was implied, was of considerable benefit to the older men. Some of those older staff members were choosing to take early retirement in order to ensure that young blood would be kept on staff, and not surprisingly they were deeply hurt by what they saw as "ungrateful" comments.

The politics of age had become a recurring theme in the Steelworkers. Senior staff and older elected leaders had never imagined that union staff layoffs would be necessary in their lifetimes, and their handling of affairs now seemed awkward and stiff. Their dismay about outspoken younger people became one dimension in the resistance to Dave Patterson's leadership as Ontario director from 1981 to 1985. The Inco strike of 1978–79 had made a national reputation for Patterson, the local union president in Sudbury, launching him as a rebel candidate for director of the Ontario district in the union elections of 1981. Certainly the personal animosity between Patterson and international president Lynn Williams had elements of intergenerational hostility on both sides. Gérard Docquier had until that point behaved as a benevolent but strict father figure in his relations with me. Later, when I declared my support for Patterson in the 1985 Ontario election Gérard's secretary Jocelyne Sévigny remarked, "Tu es un méchant garçon."

My whole social identity seemed to be in upheaval – as a man, as a young person, and as a union employee – in this convergence of gender politics and staff layoffs.

NEW TECHNOLOGY AND THE MANAGEMENT HAWKS

By 1983 my instincts were telling me to look for a safe harbour. Perhaps a run of the Facing Management course for a single local would be a good bet. What could go wrong there? A lot, it turned out.

Des Bradley was president of the Steelworkers local at Dominion Stores in Sarnia and Windsor. The stores were introducing Point Of Sale (POS) terminals, which were radically changing the work environment. On the surface, this was a tech change issue, and the local leadership requested a course to help them deal with it. While they were interested in learning about tech change, their concerns were interwoven with the other themes usually covered in the Facing Management course, including union busting and motivational psychology, among others. In particular, they wanted help from the National Office in responding to company schemes for employee involvement to change the "quality of working life."

We worked out a memo of understanding with some of Dominion's senior managers – intelligent, far-sighted, co-operative-minded people. They agreed to a significant role for the union in redesigning the workplace and took seriously the health and stress issues the union was raising. The local set up courses, acknowledging what the reorganized workplace offered to management and identifying what was in it for us.

Employees got busy working out the bugs in the new system. In brainstorming sessions we identified work positions that would need reorganization, and we reported our findings back to the company. All of us felt we had done a good job of preparing ahead of time and dealing with management when the workers needed us most – at the beginning of the change process. Their concerns about stress, speedup, and monotony were being taken seriously.

As the savings anticipated from the POS technology were beginning to be realized, sales went down for other reasons, and suddenly Dominion Stores president Conrad Black decided to cut staff by 20 per cent right through the operation. What the company did was trim all the positions that our brainstorming meetings had identified as needing reorganization. The "co-operative" work that the union had done, at both the middle and local levels in the stores, had simply resulted in a clarification of targets for management. When the company hawks made their move, they used the information that had been given to them in trust by our members.

This experience has influenced all my subsequent work in the areas of tech change and union-management co-operation. It remains a touchstone of scepticism, based not on prejudice but on bitter experience. To avoid this kind of defeat, unionists need to carefully assess the balance of forces in each situation and develop strategies accordingly. One possible strategy is to stand aside and wait for the internal contradictions of a specific workplace innovation to become evident. The risk of this approach is that in the meantime it allows the technocrats to move ahead unchallenged and to portray the union as irrelevant to the members.

My own preference is to keep the union visible as a co-operative and constructive force in the workplace. The people of goodwill in management, like those people at Dominion and many others I've worked with over the years, need to be encouraged and supported. Each time the hawks in management win out, we cannot assume that the critical consciousness of workers is thereby raised. Instead, cynicism may be increased, and the gains achieved by unions may be whittled away or simply smashed all the more easily.

By the summer of 1983 I was ready for a break. After five years of intense work I felt burned out and ready for my long-awaited study leave – the one I had negotiated in my job interview. To leave the pressures of gender politics, staff layoffs, and management betrayals for a few months of academic reflection seemed ideal. Less than ideal was another personal trauma: in August 1983 my wife Anita told me she wanted a separation after fourteen years of marriage. We spent several dismal months trying to work things out before finally, and painfully, coming to the joint decision that we each needed to do different things with our lives. In the end we amicably agreed to a divorce and to co-parenting of our two daughters.

FIVE

CIVIL WAR TIME

■ ■ ■ ■

It is not blind chance I rail at,
the flood waters that carry off
one house and leave its neighbor
standing one foot above the high
water's swirling grasp.

It is that the good go down
not easily, not gently,
not occasionally, not by random
deviation and the topple
of mischance, but almost always.

— Marge Piercy, "The Good Go Down"

A depressed Canadian Education Director returned to the Steelworkers in the fall of 1984. There was no sign that tensions in the union had abated, and I was struggling with the new experience of shared custody and with rebuilding my personal life. Through the winter I was warned that the union's 1985 elections in Ontario would be a major battle over national-ism – over U.S. control of the Canadian members – and that Canadian autonomy advocate Dave Patterson was to be the loser. I was working with Patterson from time to time, as I was with all the district directors, and when I asked him what he recommended I do in the coming year, he replied succinctly, "Duck."

DAVE PATTERSON
DIRECTOR/DIRECTEUR,
DISTRICT 6
UNITED STEELWORKERS OF AMERICA
MÉTALLURGISTES UNIS D'AMÉRIQUE
USWA
CLC-CTC

A wallet card calendar distributed in 1984-85, at the end of Dave Patterson's administration as District 6 director.

The issue of Canadian autonomy within U.S.-based unions was not new, to the Steelworkers or myself. The theme had been explored by historians (such as Irving Abella), sociologists (Bob and Jim Laxer), and political scientists (Gary Teeple). The left wing of the NDP, the Waffle, had denounced the dependency of Canadian unionism on the Americans, and the Confederation of Canadian Unions (CCU) was explicitly established to provide a safe haven for union locals that broke with their U.S. headquarters.

While Canadian autonomy was in the wind, the issue did not seem to touch me or my work directly. I was aware of the issue, of course. Just before joining the Steelworkers staff I had attended a memorial service for Kent Rowley, co-founder with Madeleine Parent of the CCU. A CCU organizer, Sarah Spinks, was a close friend throughout my Steelworker years. But it seemed to me to be an issue – one of many – that was governed by union discipline, making my own opinions on it largely irrelevant. The points on which I stood and fought during those years were more around the education program itself: the design and planning of participatory, accessible, and socially critical courses. As long as Pittsburgh did not touch those issues, I saw no reason to pick fights with the head office. And until 1985, Pittsburgh did not in any way directly interfere in my work.

Personally I had not been a strong nationalist during my years in international development education. Watching populist nationalism in Latin America during the 1960s and 1970s was enough to vaccinate me against assuming that the elites in Canada would necessarily look out for the rest of us. By joining the Steelworkers I had alienated some former friends who saw U.S.-based unions as tools of imperialism. I thought the increasing movement for Canadians to break away from U.S. control was necessary in unions like the construction trades, where headquarters control was strong, and in unions like the United Auto Workers, where Canadian representation on the international executive was limited to a single person. But in the Steelworkers four Canadian directors sat along with Lynn Williams on the International Executive Board, with over 20 per cent of the votes held in Canada. Much like Quebec in Canada's parliament, the Canadian sector worked as a bloc and indeed had provided the margin of victory in all the contested elections. Because of this I was not persuaded that the issue was urgent in the Steelworkers. Rather, I hoped to see a "natural" process of increasing Canadian autonomy in the union.

Providing representation across Canada, with offices from the Yukon to Labrador, was an expensive proposition to start with. The Canadian members demanded more service and went on strike far more frequently than the Americans did. This meant that we drew disproportionately on both the operating budget and the strike fund of the international union. Hence it was patently misleading to argue, as did the CCU and the Waffle, that Canadian dues dollars were being drained into the pockets of U.S. labour bosses.

A more subtle problem did exist, though. The ongoing subsidy from the U.S. membership generated a sense of obligation on the part of some Canadian leaders – a caution, an unwillingness to provoke arguments with the U.S. directors. This in turn played itself out in unduly timid responses when Canadian steel was being blocked from entering the U.S. market, with Canadian and U.S. members directly pitted against one another in the trade dispute.

In any case, this issue did not evolve gradually; it was posed sharply when nationalist Cec Taylor won leadership of the Stelco local in Hamilton, Local 1005, the largest local in the country in the late 1970s.[1] In alliance with Dave Patterson, then president of the Inco local in Sudbury, Taylor had linked the idea of internal democracy to the need for Canadian autonomy.

Because Cec Taylor knew me as a union democrat, he met with me several times in the early 1980s to seek my support. While I had not supported Patterson in the 1981 election for Ontario director, I treated him like all district directors once he was in. This meant active co-operation with his administration while people around me in the National Office were criticizing his alliance with Taylor and his sympathy for increased Canadian autonomy. Most interesting among the proposals discussed at that time was the idea of forming a Canadian Metalworkers Federation, which would link a Canadianized Steelworkers with a Canadianized Autoworkers and be open to other smaller unions as well. Patterson and

Leo Gerard teaching.

Autoworkers' leader Bob White both advocated this initiative, and White was keynote speaker at one of Patterson's district conferences to argue its merits. The "internationalists" argued that Patterson and Taylor favoured "breaking up" the unity of the Steelworkers, weakening the union in the face of powerful employers on both sides of the border.

Opposition to Patterson's Ontario administration was increasingly orchestrated from Pittsburgh, particularly by international secretary Lynn Williams, whose political home base was in Ontario. The other Canadian directors, along with Williams, who became International President shortly afterwards, decided to withhold co-operation from Patterson. They began to provide services to the Ontario membership directly, going around Patterson on the basis that he was not a team player. By skilful use of the levers in their hands, they were able to surround and isolate Patterson's administration. Many staff, sincerely convinced that Patterson was divisive and unpredictable, participated in undermining the director to whom they allegedly reported, and they did so with impunity knowing that the international leadership would back them in any confrontation.

In all of this I took care to give Patterson no more co-operation than I gave the other district directors, but my efforts proved to be not quite enough for the establishment team. Favourite reading for me at that time was Robert Bolt's play *A Man for All Seasons*. Like Thomas More in the play, I wanted to avoid public declarations on the issue at hand. I preferred to serve my conscience in the thickets of the mind; while working under the brambles might limit my public recognition, it was harder for the hounds to get me.

Despite this approach I found myself increasingly forced out into the open, pushed towards a blunt choice between political ethics and political survival. I thought the results of the election that had given Patterson the Ontario directorship should be respected, but this position was considered to be disloyal to the international union. By 1983 my contract with the establishment had expired. From the start I had been a protégé of Gérard Docquier, and credit for the popular "back to the locals" program had been legitimately taken by the incumbent union officers. As the shutdowns tore through the fabric of the union, the climate of optimism and outreach shifted. Within the union a mentality of "shutdown" set in – a kind of defeatism, defensiveness, and nostalgia for the glory days. In response to the membership decline in the United States, the top leaders closed ranks and channelled their energies against the internal forces of renewal.

In Quebec the response of District 5 director Clement Godbout was far more constructive. Because of the historic autonomy of Quebec he was able to maintain internal unity, revive confidence, and motivate activists to organize new members. Partly because of Lynn Williams's personal history and connections, this simply wasn't possible in Ontario. As a result the 1985 election campaign in Ontario became the focus for broader pressures.

Early in 1985 I was called into Gérard Docquier's office and asked to participate in the campaign to unseat Patterson. I asked for time to think. By that spring my options were simply to fold on my principles, as Patterson himself advised me, or to go down fighting.

At the union's Canadian Policy Conference in May, others were so busy in the internal partisan fights that they left it to me to write the policy papers.[2] I had a wonderful time. I chaired the policy committee of the union and for the first time took the platform and spoke directly to the delegates. It was the last time I was allowed to speak with the weight of the institution behind me.

By the time the conference was over the candidate who would run against Patterson had been named. After a last-minute health problem sidelined Maurice Keck, the union leadership selected a staff rep from Patterson's home local in Sudbury: my friend Leo Gerard. Leo had been hired at the same time as myself and was one of the most skilled and motivated teachers among the servicing staff. During his time in Toronto we had spent social time together and shared much as friends. Now he was the spokesperson for the Pittsburgh establishment.

HEATING UP

With six months to go before the election, partisan politics were overwhelming my little education terrain. Both candidates legitimately claimed a hand in the development and growth of the "back to the locals" program. For each scheduled course, both sides talked to me about whose supporter should be assigned to teach. In the classroom itself, supporters of Leo and Dave sat in different groups, and any participatory exercises quickly degenerated into partisan arguments. For the next six months, credit for good courses and blame for bad ones would be weapons in the battle. All the carefully constructed consensus in the union around education was coming unglued.

My neat distinction between political leadership and educational leadership was certainly "academic" in those circumstances. The week after the conference Gérard Docquier called me into his office and said that my time for fence-sitting was over. All other members of the National Office staff had declared their support for the international slate and their opposition to Dave Patterson, and Docquier insisted that I should do likewise. I told him that I would break with the national and international leadership rather than endorse the sabotage of a legitimately elected Canadian director. "We should have left you neutral," Docquier said.

That weekend was my first taste of the intensity and ambiguity that would mark the following half-year. I was taking part in a course on organizing at a hotel in Killarney, near Sudbury. During the Sunday lunch break my daughter Nyranne borrowed my union jacket and went out to the hotel pool for a swim. When she returned to the room I remembered that my car keys had been in the jacket pocket. But they weren't there any more. Nor were they anywhere along the pathway to the pool. We couldn't find them at poolside, or in the water. They had vanished. It was several anxious and frustrating hours before I was able to get help to start the car and drive out of Killarney with all the family aboard.

Certainly, there were several people at that course who were deeply upset about my political choice. I still don't know whether one of them lifted the keys to sabotage my day, or whether it was just an accident. But the line between coincidence and conspiracy had shifted for me. I had moved into a whole different kind of life, and my thoughts and fears adjusted accordingly.

Once my decision was made, I joined the Patterson group with relish at the end of regular work days. Patterson's was a ragtag army, and his leadership that of an intuitively brilliant but underresourced worker. Now I learned what it was to tackle the establishment from below. I asked for a transfer to Patterson's Ontario staff but was refused, which meant that I continued to go to work every day in the National Office surrounded by supporters of the International slate. It wasn't all bad: among those who conducted themselves with dignity in this situation was Dorothy Fisk, who worked as secretary in the Education Department by day and as secretary of Leo Gerard's campaign in the evenings. Her personal balance and professional integrity were remarkable. And during the summer vacation of 1985 I took time to participate in the play *Glow Boys*, with writer Catherine Macleod and director Don Bouzek in Kincardine and Port Elgin. The time with artists and unemployed young workers outside the union offices helped me to keep my perspective – and to improve the campaign leaflets I was writing for Dave Patterson.

COOLING OFF

Early in the fall Gérard Docquier called me in and gave me a direct assignment: I was to go to Sydney, Nova Scotia, for a week to help the local at Sydney Steel with its education needs. I phoned Winston Ruck, the staff rep in Sydney, but he was vague about what was needed. "We'll talk about it when you're here," he said. After delaying through the period of election nominations in Ontario I flew to Sydney. There each morning for a week I reported to the local office, only to be told that they were still discussing their education needs and would like me to come back the following day. It was clearly a kind of exile, a forced cooling-off period, to get me out of the way in Ontario. This rap on the knuckles for defying the establishment was one of many in those months.

Rather than railing against the unchangeable, I decided this was an opportunity for a one-week immersion course for a central Canadian. I toured the steel plant, walked the town, and tried to learn what I could about local people and conditions. Just outside the gates of Sydney Steel I found a perfect study location: the "lunch" counter, open day and night to catch all the shifts. It carried every possible variety both of potato chips and of what some people in 1985 still called girlie magazines. By the cash register was the program for harness racing at Tartan Downs and that season's feature, a shelf full of Hallowe'en masks.

At the lunch counter I met Terry Crawley, who warned me against the food, ordered a coffee, and slowly let the tension of a day's work drain out. As I got to know him I found out that Terry was – and still is – a verbal scrapper who often ruffled the feathers of others in the local union. At one point, he was president of the Cape Breton Labour Council, where there was more room for his outspoken style than in most local union meetings.

"There's still a knot in my stomach," he said that first day at the lunch counter. "Ever since Black Friday. A knot of fear, that's been in all of us for a generation now. Surviving week-to-week. You can't imagine what that does to a community."

Behind his fear was anger. On Black Friday, in 1967, the company announced it would close the steel plant, the main employer in Sydney. The workers, their families, and the community never recovered. Several piecemeal and expensive rescue efforts failed to make the plant socially and economically viable. By 1985 even people with Terry's drive and ability were finding it hard to imagine shaping their own futures.

In the autumn the area still had a lively tourist trade, though the big buses tended to skirt the city, taking in the fall colours of the Cabot Trail and showering U.S. dollars on handicraft stores. For the people who lived in Sydney, there was no public sports arena in 1985, and the radio station was closing. The huge new building for the local newspaper was only one-third occupied, and the night life had gone back into people's kitchens. The city's economic decline was accelerated by the gradual closing of the coal mines as well as by the slow decline of the fishing industry.[3]

The people were proud, dignified, and talented, but poor. The poverty was different than in Newfoundland or Saskatchewan, because this place had once had a taste of real prosperity in the coal and steel boom at the beginning of the century. Just as the people were whetting their appetite, the plates were snatched out from under their noses. Sydney was at the centre of the world map in 1903, but by 1985 it was on the edge.

As a Cape Bretoner, Terry knew this story in his bones. As a union leader, he had got used to explaining it to people from away. He himself moved through the union education structure to graduate from the two-month residential course at the Labour College of Canada, a residential program that provides social science courses at a first-year university level to emerging trade union leaders. Now located at the University of Ottawa and sponsored by the Canadian Labour Congress, the Labour College offers the most lengthy and advanced course provided under the direct control of the labour movement. Participants are usually sponsored by their affiliate and by a series of scholarships to help pay for much of the lost income and expenses associated with the program. The course helped Terry face the succession of undermotivated managers who were presiding over the slow decline of his workplace.

As we talked, I was uncomfortably aware of how much I must resemble those managers in his eyes. I was from Hamilton, a steel city more favoured in the new "restructured" Canada. And I would be moving on from Sydney to another community at the end of my week of forced exile. But Terry was courteous. He asked me to drop by his house later on, after he had done some paperwork at the union hall.

I filled in the time with an errand, taking my electric teapot in for repair. One of the constants in the recent series of hotel rooms, the teapot had bounced around in my suitcase once too often. Behind the counter the manager smoothed her apron, smiled briskly, and listened attentively to the problem. Stoop-shouldered, she pushed aside a box of light switches and laid out her treasure – a Toronto yellow pages. With it, she could phone for replacement parts, for appliances made in the States and repaired in central Canada. It would take three weeks to receive the part. By then I would be back in Toronto myself. This was the hinterland.[4]

Terry's home was on the pier next to the mill. In his kitchen that evening we talked about the community, the employer, but mostly about the union. After all, that's what we could both touch, both try to reshape.

In Sydney, to drink in that kitchen, to look into that hardware store, to sit in that lunch counter, is to know the hollowness of most policy discussion about "economic planning." The voices of towns like Sydney are not heard in the standard economic policy circles. Planning implies some control over the flow of money in and the flow of money out; it seemed to me that individually and collectively, the workers in Sydney had neither.[5] "Economic restructuring" has an antiseptic ring to it, but during the early 1980s it was a gun pointed at Canadian workers.

I felt then and I still feel today that Canadian labour has a responsibility to cushion the fall for its members and other workers hurt by economic restructuring. And as the case of Cape Breton makes clear, unions need to propose ways of creating employment and mobilizing local capital so that resources are not increasingly concentrated in a few large cities.

Back in Ontario, unity and responsibility were not the order of the day in 1985. All the energy among Ontario Steelworkers was committed to fighting one another. And the might of the international union was focused on driving out a voice for internal democracy and Canadian autonomy.

After I returned from Cape Breton, more angry and determined than before, my hardest moment came in late fall at the Ontario Federation of Labour convention. I drafted a personal statement about union democracy and the Patterson election, typing in the title "To Steelworker friends" at the top. As Steelworker delegates filed out of the meeting hall at noon, I handed a copy to each one. In part, I stated:

> All along, I've done my best to keep partisan politics out of membership education. Respecting the verdict of the members in the last election, I worked with all three district directors to build the skills and information our members need to handle employers effectively. Throughout the past year, I was being told that my neutrality would no longer be tolerated. I was expected to join the attack on Dave Patterson's administration. . . . I think it's time for our union to stop bickering and get back to the job of representing the members. . . . While Dave Patterson has made mistakes during this time, he isn't the only one. It is cynical and misleading to scapegoat him for the reverses we have suffered. . . . The continuing effort to isolate Dave from the members who elected him has failed. It has also discredited those who conducted it.[6]

When Gérard Docquier walked by, I handed him the sheet. Then came my colleagues from the National Office. I eventually gave out more than two hundred copies of the sheet, directly, personally, hand to hand. At one point, when I was physically wavering, the president of a major local within the union put his arm around my back, propping me up as I went through one of the most nerve-wracking experiences of my life.

Three weeks later Patterson was defeated in the election. The predictions in May had been of 15 per cent support for Patterson and 85 per cent for the Pittsburgh candidate, Leo Gerard. But we gave them a run for their money, and in the end Patterson was only defeated 60–40. Ironically, it was the relatively close vote that sealed my fate. Had the result been a landslide, I might have been kept around as window dressing. But 40 per cent of the vote against the concentrated weight of the international machine represented a tangible threat. It was not to be taken lightly.

Once again I was called into Gérard Docquier's office, where I was surprised to see my text "To Steelworker friends" displayed prominently on his desk. Among other things, Docquier said that he no longer saw me as head of education in the union. The meeting was followed by a stream of correspondence between him and me. I got a letter accepting my "resignation." I sent one protesting that I had not resigned, and then I lodged a grievance. The grievance was handled by fellow staff members who were key actors in the sabotage of Dave Patterson's administration and the defeat of Canadian autonomy in the election. In the end I got a settlement of a couple of weeks' pay, after eight years of service.

In this process it became clear that my ability to put my job on the line was strengthened by my professional training, which meant I could get a job elsewhere, either in the union movement or outside. This situation of relative privilege is like that of skilled journeymen in industrial plants, people like plumbers and electricians who are able to press back against arbitrary supervisors because they have more work options than assembly workers who lack such formal and portable credentials. Certainly the fact that I had other employment options, and better paying ones at that, strengthened my resolve at this critical time ... and no doubt reinforced the uneasiness of the Steelworkers leadership about "academics."

My feeling then – and still today – is that with the plant closings and layoffs of 1981–82 the Steelworkers union lost its vision and nerve. For the next few years all that counted was "loyalty" – not to principles but to the strategies and alliances of Lynn Williams in his run for power. During that time, increasingly, I became distanced from Gérard Docquier and the other insiders by refusing to play partisan games amidst my work in the education program.

Because of the past closeness between Docquier and I, the battle had become highly personal, and it would be years before we could look each other in the eye again. My dismissal closed the "civil war time" of my life. In a central political battle, it had turned out that the educational leader could not be a conscientious objector. In the end I fought rather than caved in on my principles, and I have never regretted that decision.

So what was the big deal, anyway? Why take a stand on this issue, when I had compromised on so many others? Obviously, many decent trade unionists had decided that the election was about personalities and opted for Leo Gerard because of his known capacity for consensus building and strategy. It must have seemed to many that Dave Patterson's more individualistic rebel style would be less effective in the leadership position. Others simply shrugged and decided to let this one pass.

But for me the issue was union democracy, an issue that went to the core of my reasons for working in the union movement. And, like so many others, I had to "learn democracy through the exercise of democracy; for that knowledge, above all others, can only be assimilated experientially."[7]

Although a union may be a less than perfect place for working-class people to experience democracy, keeping the institution aligned with its political rhetoric is important. After all, schools are an imperfect site for learning, and organized religion an imperfect garden for cultivating spirituality. But if learning matters, or spirituality matters, the practice of either of them should be defended most ardently in the institutions that most claim to embody their essence. The odds are better there than in society at large, and the terrain should not be given up without a fight. The same goes for democracy in unions.

In this case, democracy had clearly been flouted. Time after time Dave Patterson had been overruled on basic administrative decisions. One special irony for me came when Pittsburgh refused to confirm his appointment of staff because they were "outsiders" to the union – while headquarters went on blithely ignoring the many "outsiders," including me, who were already on the payroll. As Patterson's budgets were restricted and his staff assigned directly from the National Office, his electoral demise was gleefully anticipated by those staff loyal to the union establishment. I was upset about it, but I held my tongue and did my job, at least until I was cornered and had to make a move.

The democracy I am committed to is tangible in a union. It means that twenty or thirty workers take seriously their right to elect a steward from among themselves. They encourage the most capable and honest person to take the position, and then they hold that representative accountable to defend and inform them. At the local union, workers ensure that no clique runs away with their resources or credibility, and they remind officers that the local meeting is the final authority in all decisions. In relations with the employer, they refuse to be divided or cowed, ensuring that a good contract is achieved and that it is enforced through the grievance procedure. In union courses, they keep the instructor on track and insist that their needs for relevant content and participatory process are met. When they vote for a senior officer of the union, as they did for Patterson, they expect their vote to be respected, not second-guessed by career union politicians.

While this ideal pattern is not always found in union life, it appears more often there than in the workplaces where members earn their livings. And when workers band together in their workplace to organize or sustain a union, they want to keep it clear from capricious and power-hungry behaviour. When these expectations are betrayed, they may protest or retreat into cynicism, but they should not find their educational leader actively supporting the betrayal. So when I was told that Docquier had secured the explicit support of twenty-two of the National Office staff, I decided I could not be the twenty-third.

If I were more of a theorist, my break point might have come over the fine points in a policy paper. If I were more of a nationalist, I might have consciously worked from within to promote a break with Pittsburgh. If I were more of a negotiator, I might have put all my weight behind a particular strike. But at the core I am a radical democrat, and when I was ordered to defend the sabotage of an elected union leader I just couldn't do it.

When the word hit the grapevine, reactions were mixed. Most of my co-workers treated me with respect. One colleague spread the word that I had lost my mental balance and was imagining bomb threats against my family. Another wrote to say that he had heard me "branded as everything from a traitorous radical to an anti-establishment pinko" and remarked that I was "doing it the hard way." A third offered emotional and practical support in my grievance, adding, "Your time will come to make a wrong right."

■ ■ ■ ■

During that period, among other things I found out how politically charged union education is. That is why the alert union leader pays special attention to what goes on in courses. From the course participants, ideas are generated every day; from the leadership there is a steady flow of statements, only some of which are captured in union publications.

The traffic of ideas within the labour movement follows many routes, and at some intersections educators are to be found. We select and shape messages to be passed in a climate of trust between leaders and members. Every day a union educator has to make choices about the ideas to amplify and those to muffle, going both ways. This double accountability works well as long as the distance between members and leaders is not too great. As these conditions eroded at the Steelworkers in the early 1980s, so too did the possibilities of the intermediary role.

In this sense, the democratic educator in a union has a "political agenda." While the explicit themes of my work as union educator had been centred around issues such as facing management or women's rights, the subtext, which came more and more into focus during the "civil war time," was about participation in shaping the union and the society.

In this time I tasted new possibilities and limitations in the union educator role. At times, as something that seems unsettlingly close to court jesters, we are expected to present unpalatable truths in an entertaining manner; as long as our influence is not too visible, we can speak clearly to the monarch without fear of having our heads lopped off. As cabaret performers, we must hold the attention of course participants and keep bringing in fresh material, or the show will be shut down. At different times the union educator is required to be all these things: go-between, court jester, and cabaret performer. But in the end, each of us has to live with ourselves, apart and united, *solitaire et solidaire*.

After this defeat I was bitter for a while, disappointed in friends who I felt had let me down or who had attacked me behind my back. Even now I still feel an anger that flares out when I see a betrayal of union democracy, and to me, this is a healthy – indeed, absolutely necessary – anger.

The Steelworkers' civil war was fought in front of the entire Ontario labour movement. When I first declared my support for Dave Patterson, a senior staff person from another union called to say, "We have a parking spot set aside for you at our office." After the result was clear, other unions approached me to work with them. The most attractive to me was the Communications and Electrical Workers of Canada (CWC).

It seemed fitting that the CWC's Ontario headquarters was located in the Steelworkers' downtown Toronto building. To get to the CWC office I had to walk up the stairs and past the USWA office where staff had bitterly criticized me during the Patterson campaign. On March 1, 1986 – eight years exactly after I had begun my union work with the Steelworkers – I made that trip up the stairs to begin my first day on the job as education representative at the CWC.

SIX

BACK TO BASICS: GRASSROOTS CAMPAIGNS, POWER, AND ART

■ ■ ■ ■

Superficial things change,
as do profound things,
ways of thinking change,
along with everything else in this world
and so it should be no surprise
that I myself am changing.

– Mercedes Sosa, "Todo Cambia"[1]

In the spring of 1987, at noon on the third and final day of a course for local union officers, I was heading from the seminar room towards the luncheon buffet. As usual my head was full of thoughts, not about food, but about how we would start off the afternoon's program.

As I crossed the lawn behind the hotel where we were meeting, I saw two union members who had not shown up for class that morning. When they didn't arrive I had asked someone to phone their rooms. We found out that they were still celebrating after a late-night card game. Each had apparently won several hundred dollars, and they were not planning to attend class.

The two "truants" cheerfully called me over, still slightly drunk. I said hello and dutifully reminded them that I would have to report them as absent for the day. This meant that they would lose a day's wages.

"Of course, D'Arcy, you have to do your job," one of them said. "Anyway, we each won more than a day's wages at cards."

The other piped in: "You're lucky we didn't show up, because in the shape we're in we would have fucked up the class completely."

"No hard feelings, then?" I asked.

"No hard feelings. Have a beer."

So I sat with them and had a beer. It was a sunny spring day, and we chatted quietly about travel, family, and their employer. After a few minutes I handed them my empty bottle and stood to leave.

"It was a really interesting course, D'Arcy. Thanks."

My feelings were mixed as I walked away. Part of me envied these two men their freedom and their refusal to confer any special power on me. Another part resented the fact that they weren't meeting my effort half way, since I had prepared hard for that course. I had brought together officers from two CWC locals, both of which represented employees of the same company and had never been comfortable together. There had been plenty of friction between the "cowboy" local and the "responsible" local, and the performance by this pair of cowboys would not help bring the two locals closer together. Yet the clash on the lawn – if you could call it that – had been frank and without rancour.

In a way that experience jelled something for me. Around that time I had begun reflecting more systematically on how union work is necessarily embedded in broader power dynamics – especially the overriding power of management vs. the intricate play of power within the union. There were all types of potential textbook power at play in this union situation: from "coercive power," based on fear of punishment; through "information power," based on the leader's possession of information that others see as necessary or valuable; to "reward power," based on a leader's ability to provide rewards for other people – positive incentives such as pay, promotion, or recognition.[2] These and other types of power work in complex ways, especially within unions.

The truants knew, for instance, that I could report them to their local and recommend that they not be paid for the third day of the course – an example of "coercive power." But they also probably knew that if I did report them, their local could always decide to ignore my recommendation. And my very *closeness* to the two truants influenced my capacity to exercise this power. As well as drinking an illicit beer together on a lawn we shared not only a continuing commitment to unionism but also even our gender, race, and approximate age and income level.

I also had the power of "information" at my fingertips. If I had prepared and designed the course effectively, the most significant judges would be the other participants in the course. If I established the value of the information I was providing in the course, the other participants would consider that the two truants were actually missing something, and they would feel the pressure of this on their behaviour. This was possibly my greatest advantage over the truants.

My "reward power" was effectively neutralized because the two truants had already secured an amount of money equivalent to their wages in the card game. Indeed, their status in the group as a result of winning the card game may have given them the capacity to mock or challenge my leadership.

In the end neither the two truants nor I put our power bases to the test. Instead, we acknowledged a standoff and took pleasure in each other's decision not to push the challenge further. I reported their absence matter of factly, without trying to make an example of them, and they didn't try to promote a rebellion against me. It goes to show, perhaps, that a course leader's power is always limited, always subject not only to resistance but also to negotiation. While unionists limit the arbitrary exercise of management power in the workplace, they also limit their leaders and their educators in exercising power within the union.

For adult educators, the recognition of these limits is significant. The literature is full of exhortation to the educator to avoid imposing on the adult learner. For a radical thinker such as Paulo Freire, this issue is a central concern. Studies of adult learning also stress that people, as individuals, can exercise at least some control over their learning, that while attendance can be coerced, learning cannot. In the union culture the matter is not settled by either the intent of an individual educator or the will of an individual learner. Rather, a collective dynamic limits the educator's power. The checks and balances within the labour movement create particular conditions for learning and teaching, and adult educators committed by temperament and ideology to democratic practice will be attracted to these aspects of the union culture.

STARTING OVER AT THE CWC

When I joined the Communications and Electrical Workers of Canada in 1986 it had grown nearly ten times from its membership of four thousand in the early 1970s. The CWC had separated from the Communications Workers of America in an amicable divorce in the early 1970s and had begun organizing as an autonomous Canadian union, mainly from its base in Saskatchewan and with a few members at Northern Telecom in

Ontario. It was still relatively small, but it was growing, Canadian, and democratic – the "tiny perfect union."

In the late 1970s the cwc began going after employees in the other telephone companies, from Newfoundland to Manitoba, and within a decade had organized most of them. As well the union moved beyond telephone workers by merging, in 1984, with the International Union of Electrical, Radio and Machine Workers (iue), an organization of industrial workers who produced components and equipment for telecommunications and the electrical and electronic sector of Canadian industry.

After the merger with the iue, cwc membership varied between thirty-five thousand and forty thousand depending on economic conditions. In

Ed Seymour, union educator and labour historian, who brought me into the cwc.

Ontario the union's fifteen thousand members consisted of a Telecommunications Sector, mostly employed at Bell Canada, and an Industrial Sector including employees from the former iue. The two sectors met together every September and March, with education consistently on the agenda. Ed Seymour, the cwc's skilled, long-time union educator, had hired me to fill the place he had vacated when he was elected the union's Ontario vice-president.

My new job was different from my Steelworkers position, at once narrower and broader. As before, my core responsibility was to plan, design, and facilitate courses for members, primarily those elected to representative positions such as steward or local union officer. I was the only full-time education person in the cwc, and the secretary working with me had responsibility for at least three other reps as well. There was a handful of local union instructors prepared by Ed Seymour, but most of the time, if I wanted something to happen, I had to do it myself.

This meant deciding where a course was needed, arranging the details, and letting the potential participants know about it. I would pack up the participant kits, manuals, and video playback unit and travel out to the course location – in places from Gananoque to Hamilton, from Owen

Sound to Sudbury. Usually a course would run for three days, with eight hours of formal class time and optional evening sessions. This "back to the basics" grassroots education could be extremely tiring, at times constricting, but it was also full of potential and satisfaction.

Like all reps working in the CWC, I was given locals to service: I handled membership meetings, grievances, and arbitrations in the Hamilton-Niagara area. For six months I worked full-time in an organizing drive. And along the way I was given ad hoc assignments, such as co-ordinating the union's part in the national campaign against the Goods and Services Tax (GST) or helping build links with counterpart unions in Mexico during the lead-up to the North American Free Trade Agreement (NAFTA).

My job, in general, was to help build a CWC identity and a system for sustaining that new identity. It felt a bit like the kind of opportunity that had given birth to the "back to the locals" campaign at the Steelworkers. In short order we developed a "working classes" campaign in the Industrial Sector and a "grassroots campaign" in the Telecommunications Sector. Together these projects became the motor for CWC education, under the slogan "Thinking Union."

WORKING CLASSES AND A GRASSROOTS CAMPAIGN

After the harshness of my final year with the Steelworkers, I had a vivid sense of the forces that could impede the kind of work I liked to do in a union. Certain forces in particular seemed to work closely together: negative media, hostile managements, and internal resisters. As a union educator I had experience with all three, and in my new situation I was determined to handle the problems more effectively and especially to ensure that they didn't combine to pose an impossible block to my work.

The negative media image of unions worked to undermine the confidence of union members in the capacity of their organizations to address the future. U.S. television, the medium that most pervades Canada, rarely depicts working-class people or the unions they have built, preferring instead the rich and famous. The unionists who do appear are most often depicted as an obstacle to progress or a source of thuggery and stupidity.[3] These images weaken organized working people's sense of dignity and add to a sense of powerlessness in the labour movement – creating in turn an immediate obstacle in union education. Course participants become less open, union leaders become less hopeful of change, and the curiosity and risk-taking required in transformational learning become diminished.

The offensive by employers to destroy unions works alongside the negative media and is, if anything, even more harsh. The techniques of union busting – to divide and conquer, avoid collective representation, build a false "teamwork" loyalty – are elements of an integrated management campaign for a "union-free" environment.[4] This offensive can be extremely dangerous to critical union education. Further, it reinforces a tendency to avoid opening up our internal processes. Precisely at the time when we need more open union-sponsored conferences to discuss social problems and policy alternatives, the union-free offensive strengthens the siege mentality in unions and distances us from potential allies.

Within unions, a resistance to change and a penchant for internal bickering form the other closely related force. While other institutions seem to constantly fall in love with their own rhetoric, they may be less vulnerable, more able to afford it. Rather than clinging to dogmas that have outlived their usefulness, unions need boldness in addressing the rapid and comprehensive changes in the workplace. But internal political rivalries weaken our ability to speak with one voice and reinforce a limiting sense of caution.

My experience in the Steelworkers had left me burned, sensitive to the possibility that these forces might again become aligned in ways that would overwhelm my work and hurt me personally. Yet I found that by specifically tracing the sources of resistance rather than avoiding them or lumping them together, I was able to maintain a sense of direction.

In Ontario, two-thirds of cwc members worked at Bell Canada, mostly as telephone operators and technicians. After the merger with the iue, a third of the Ontario membership worked in manufacturing plants, including Mitsubishi in Midland, where they made television tubes, Inglis in Cambridge, where they made clothes dryers, or General Electric in Oakville, where they made light bulbs. The telecommunications members were not just more numerous but also more highly educated and culturally homogeneous than the industrial membership. They were also better paid and more secure in their jobs.

When I joined the cwc staff in March 1986, the union had already scheduled a course for officers of the Industrial Sector locals. I took part in that course with Peter Klym, who was one of the builders of the cwc and had recently stepped down as vice-president for the Ontario Region. I found that working with the Industrial Sector members was not that different from working with the Steelworker members who came from metal manufacturing plants, and as I talked with them about the challenge of involving new people in the life of the union an idea began to take shape. Gradually, it grew into a "Working Classes" education campaign, which lasted for over a year.

Like the "back to the locals" program started in the Steelworkers eight years earlier, this initiative required careful mustering of support – political, financial, and personal. The political support came from the vice-president of the Industrial Sector, Glenn Pattinson. The personal support came from a small team of five people: Linda McKenzie-Nicholas, vice-president of Local 534 at the Complax plant in Cobourg, and Jim Counahan, president of Local 532 at the Mitsubishi plant in Midland; Carole Condé and Karl Beveridge, artists I had worked with on a Radio Shack project at the Steelworkers; and Matthew Sanger, a graduate student in educational theory who shared my interest in literacy work.

Our six-person team researched the learning needs of the members by making workplace visits, holding meetings with activists, and circulating a questionnaire to all members. We designed and conducted courses, particularly "Facing Management" courses. We worked at building discussion among local union leaders in a way that encouraged their participation.

Still, the educational challenge was quite different from that of the Steelworkers' "back to the locals" program. By this time the local leaders were facing an integrated offensive by employers in the electrical and electronic manufacturing sector. The workers experienced this as increased insecurity in their jobs – and, for some of them, job loss. In general companies were staging a redefining of the workplace, and the result was a continually engineered sense of anxiety in the workplace.[5] All this was in the context of the push to dismantle the industry in Canada as part of the Free Trade Agreement with the United States.[6]

The survey questionnaire responses indicated a low level of information about the union and a high degree of alienation from the local leadership. The union was largely inactive in providing programs in training for job skills, particularly in regard to new technologies, and the survey showed there was a strong need in this area. We discussed these results extensively with leaders at the local, regional, and national level and out of this shaped a framework for an ongoing educational program. This involved membership courses and a push for job training that produced the Sectoral Skills Council.

With the member survey completed and an arts display and a booklet called *Class Work* produced, the campaign itself ended in late 1988. The other members of the team moved onto other things, and I began to build on the project. Whereas at the start of the Steelworkers "back to the locals" initiative the union culture had been unfamiliar and my reputa-

Wayne Marston, president of Local 42 of CEP, which represents Bell Canada workers in Hamilton, takes the microphone at the Ontario Council meeting of the union. Wayne worked with me through the 1988 strike at Bell Canada and was instrumental in negotiating government funds to set up the Ontario Workers Arts and Heritage Centre in Hamilton in 1995. Behind him are Rocklee Johns of London and Chris King of Windsor.

tion in union circles non-existent, this time I could draw on knowledge, networks, and understandings established over the past eight years.

Because we based our agenda for the educational work on the survey results, the work flowed directly from the membership – and this in turn enhanced the standing of Industrial Sector local activists. The "Class Work" display and booklet prepared by Carole Condé and Karl Beveridge circulated through regional meetings, union courses, and wider events in the labour movement, and the issues it explored became more familiar to CWC members whose working experience had often been exclusively at a telephone company. The educational campaign helped to strengthen initiatives like health and safety and grievance handling, which had been losing momentum.

At the same time I had to make sure to balance my work in the Industrial Sector against work with the two-thirds of the membership in tele-

An image from the visual series "Class Work" by Karl Beveridge and Carole Condé. The artists made an exception from their usual practice and included two non-professional actors. Seated on the left is Linda Mackenzie-Nicholas and standing behind her is Jim Counahan. These two local union officers were key allies in building grassroots education in the CWC.

communications. For this majority of the members I continued the programs of steward and officer training that my predecessor Ed Seymour had established. I also became engaged in the "grassroots campaign," which involved union staff meeting directly with every local union officer and steward to spend about half a day reviewing developments in the telecommunications industry, looking at the potential impact of the changes on both members and union. These activists would then meet one on one with the members they represented, seeking opinions and sharing information. They would pass out a brief questionnaire, and the responses would be tabulated to guide union action in the future. Indeed, with the new technologies being introduced, with the shifts in economic structure and heated political debates about the status of telecommunications as a public service or a traded commodity, the sector provided an echo chamber for many of the other changes under way in the society.[7]

The grassroots campaign started from the issue of job security and considered the potential impact of various changes on the quality and continuity of work experience. From the leadership's perspective, the broad context was that of deregulation – the retreat of public authorities from the idea of telecommunications as a public good to be held publicly accountable. The campaign material asked for member input on issues of tech change, job security, occupational stress, and customer service.

The union was responding first to the fact that large business users were advancing their own needs in telecommunications policy. Those users saw telecommunications not as a public utility but as a potential source of profit and of social and economic power. Further, the arena of telecommunications had shifted. In the past, publishing, broadcasting, and telecommunications were distinct economic sectors, and now they were merging. In this situation the union required a new kind of internal conversation rather than the traditional debate on collective bargaining priorities and interpretation of contract language. The "grassroots campaign" aimed to expand this new conversation.

The union undertook to publicly challenge the corporate agenda, which our studies showed would increase profits in this sector in Canada through higher prices for consumers and a decline in access and service quality. To convert what had, for the most part, been previously seen as a utility under public control into a zone for unrestricted private speculation, the corporate sector was pushing for long distance competition, local measured service, rate rebalancing, and harmonization with U.S. standards. The union had to not only lobby government on these issues but also keep its membership engaged in the issues. The role of the grassroots campaign was to ensure that we had broad and informed involvement by local union activists as the union moved into the public forum.

ANGER AND THE ARTISTIC CHALLENGE

When participants do rebel in union courses this can be a reflection of accumulated anger and pain from their class standing in the society and the workplace. Donna Robinson, a former president of Local 51, Communications and Electrical Workers of Canada, a feminist and a poet, speaks of the knot of anger in her stomach, and the fear behind it:

Anger pours
like coffee in a cup,
tasting warm and bitter,
the steam rising
directionless
in the open air.
Inside,
another click,
another minute in another endless day.[8]

In her poems Donna, a telephone operator living in Ottawa, brings out the truth behind the jobs in the "new" high-tech sector. The phone operators she works with have migraines, repetitive strain injuries, deteriorating eyesight, and nervous depressions. These are induced directly by the "underload" that they have experienced over years on a job that became increasingly machine-paced, monotonous, and fragmented.

In industrial workplaces the visible strain of production is on the spinal column, while the invisible damage penetrates the lungs. In information-age workplaces like Donna's, the load falls on the central nervous system. But just as ergonomics has been able to redesign a heavy lifting job to minimize the damage to workers' backs, so too could engineering redesign the job of the phone operator to be more diverse, self-controlled, and interesting – if the companies were so willing.

But in 1988 the country's largest phone company, Bell Canada, dug in its heels on this and other issues, and the members reacted by declaring a strike. The vote in favour of going out on strike was only 51.3 per cent, providing a dangerously weak mandate, yet we kept going for seventeen weeks in two hundred communities across Ontario and Quebec. Less than 1 per cent of the members crossed the picket line. In the end the union was $6 million in debt with a depleted strike fund, and we were all exhausted. Several millions of dollars needed to be repaid to other unions who helped see us through. Was it all worth it? The verdict, aptly stated by Diane McLachlan, president of the Orillia, Ontario, local, was, "We didn't bring Ma Bell to her knees, but we sure as hell made her curtsy."

From the start of the strike Don Bouzek had been videotaping members about their experience, with myself and Denise Norman, another rep, as co-ordinators. We all wanted the members' voices to be central to the final tape, using union leaders and actors only if necessary to complement the perspective brought by rank and filers. Our best footage was of a technician talking about how he had enjoyed the strike.

Member at work in CWC workplace.

One of the technician's stories was about a time when the local police were called to clear pickets away from a Bell building in a small Ontario town. About forty police officers gathered across the street and were forming up to take charge of the situation. At a prearranged signal the strikers scattered, leaving the police in tidy ranks to defend property against a non-existent "threat," in full view of the public and a union photographer. This was Keystone Cops stuff, and according to the union guy on the video, the strikers had a ball with it.

Within minutes the strikers were back on the road, practising "zone defence" on the managers' repair vehicles: they were letting each and every customer know that the manager responding to their call was stealing a striker's job. Meanwhile the big shots at Bell Canada decided whether or not to summon the police again. It was war of manoeuvre versus war of position.

On camera the technician Don had interviewed was lucid, vivid, and funny. But shortly after the return to work he lost his job, as one of a series of strike leaders picked out to be "disciplined" by Bell. The union staff representative, trying to get the technician's job back, said this was no time for the worker to appear in a public video visibly displaying his defiance of the employer. We couldn't use the footage.

The decision bothered me. I was embarrassed to acknowledge that the CWC, one of the most dynamic and respected unions in the Canadian labour movement, was so weak that it had to hide a worker's true feelings to protect that worker. This decision was not an artistic choice, but a political choice – a simple judgement of the balance of forces between employer and union.

Don cut out his best footage to protect the member, telling me later that I had been more upset than he was. He knew the union had limited funds after the strike, and he didn't want to push things. For him and the others at Ground Zero Productions, it was no big deal. Instead they taped an actor telling some of the stories the striker had recounted. This meant that the sequence became a story *about* a strike rather than showing what happened *within* a strike. For me, while the video may have gained other qualities through good dramatization, it seemed that the story lost the immediacy and authenticity of the first-person voice.

In this case the union had to count on the empathy of the artist, and the situation, I think, reveals the finer points about the relationship between unions and art. Individuals of great passion, eloquence, and creativity can be found within union culture. But developing the collective imagination in unions requires momentum and modelling, and labour-positive professional artists are essential elements in kick-starting and coaching along this process.

In Canada labour-positive artists, a minority in their own communities, have played a crucial role in strengthening labour's side in the politics of perception. The process usually begins with a specific project, such as the video docu-drama *Re-Connecting*. Sometimes a union takes the initiative and contracts artists to carry it out. On other occasions artists obtain arts funding for a proposal and approach a union for support and guidance. In both cases the terms of alliance have to be clearly negotiated. As a first step, unionists must begin to take artists seriously as workers.

Artists, understandably, tend to apply union principles to their encounter with the trade union movement as an employer. They resent being used as pawns in internal union feuds not of their own making. And they are critical of union budgeting practices that place a low priority on artists' work. Even artists who consider themselves to be "progressive" or "militant" often experience a conflict around their role. As filmmaker

Laura Sky puts it: "Often, because of the economic insecurity we face, we are tempted to compensate by 'buying' the position that being artists affords us – the egotism of it – the specialness of it. It's a part of ourselves that we don't like to admit."[9]

The frustration of artists who have negative experiences with unions is not that a major market is closed to them. The "union market" is unlikely to be of commercial significance to any but a handful of artists. But they look to the labour movement as a possible model of work relations that could be applied to other parts of the cultural economy. According to Sky, for instance, they are also looking for a kind of *connectedness*, "an effectiveness with the forces of change in our country. We want to be able to contribute to the winning of a better life – for artists and workers alike. We understand clearly the necessity and the immense satisfaction that are inherent in developing a connectedness with all people who are fighting these fights."

Early childhood activism in Hamilton during the 1988 CWC *strike against Bell Canada.*

The arts community carries its own internal cross-currents and pressures. Artists have to deal with government funders, consultants, and commercial dealers. The arts producers themselves include different disciplines, all intercut by age, gender, and race. The arts scene has its own difficulties with the interplay of competition and often malicious conflict. In a sector of scarcity, rivalries are not polite – after all, it is unlikely that the loser in an arts run-off will be appointed to the Senate. Within this politic, progressive artists have a difficult job to do. They expect union activists to respect them for what they do, and to support them when they voice their own needs. For pro-labour artists, the Independent Artists' Union's slogan of "a living culture, a living wage" captured their two primary goals. Without a vibrant arts scene, there is no context for individual creativity. With continental forces operating in the mainstream image factory, progressive artists need all the allies they can find – including those in the labour movement.

But while most unionists would agree with adding creativity to the list of worker entitlements, placing a priority on cultural politics is another matter. In the most privileged parts of union institutions, one can hear the argument that artists are a waste of time, and that what unions should do is simply buy the mainstream talents available on the market. Following this perspective, it makes sense for a major union to have its design work done by the same agency that handles Purina Dog Chow.

Artists often approach unions with an inflated sense of labour's relative wealth in financial and organizational resources. It sometimes seems difficult for artists to understand and respect the habits of collectivity in union work and the dynamics of the union culture around participation and voluntarism. Their hard-won "independence" from corporate sponsorship and their negotiated "arms-length" relation to government funding do little to promote sympathy with the slow and informal processes of accountability and discipline in trade union life.

When unions raise concerns about content, artists sometimes see this as censorship or authoritarianism. Some artists have a hard time feeling comfortable in the collective ethos of the labour movement. And sometimes artists have difficulty presenting their needs in a form intelligible within the union culture – for example, by linking the arts to other social entitlements, such as health care, for which unionists have fought on behalf of all working people. The arts community is not immune to the anti-union prejudices current in society as a whole.

When artists and unionists meet properly, the result is greater than the sum of the parts. We all reconnect with the passion that got us into questioning the conventional wisdom in the first place. The artistic drive – like the organizing drive and the strike – has provided new learning experiences for myself and others in the union. And both the "Working Classes" campaign and the "Grassroots" campaign had placed education front and centre. The knowledge, confidence, and skills of local activists were the focus of reflection by elected officials and staff alike. For me politically, all of these campaigns were an indicator of the health of the union. For me personally they were an invitation to stretch my capacities, to put my heart into the job with the sense that the work might really make a difference.

After the Bell Canada strike, with limited time and resources local union course leaders were at best only able to sustain the formal courses already in place. New initiatives had to be temporarily set aside. I took a study leave and wrote the first draft of this book. When I returned six months later I found the leadership engaged less in grassroots education and more on matters of public policy that affected the union. It was time for me to move as well from the basic activism courses to the interplay of "stakeholders" in the restructuring of Canada's labour market.

SEVEN

POLICY TIME ON THE JOB
TRAINING FRONT

■ ■ ■ ■

An adult education structure is a project in action, living at the
rhythm of the situation that gives it life. This project usually results
from negotiation, from compromises that must take into consideration divergent interests and conflicting goals. The program is produced
by social relations that do not cease to exist after it is established, whose
tensions and contrary points of view can always return to challenge
and modify it later.

    – Gérard Malglaive, *Enseigner à des Adultes: Travail et Pédagogie*

One night in December 1989, CWC president Fred Pomeroy had insom-
nia. As a result he stayed up for hours painstakingly reading a draft report
on job training, which was to be reviewed the next day at a meeting of the
Ontario Premier's Council on Technology.

Around that time labour-policy researchers had become increasingly
focused on the growing split between "good jobs" and "bad jobs."[1] Across
North America the number of middle-level jobs had shrunk after 1975
under the pressures of tech change, changing demographic patterns, and
shifts in the economic base. Canada was moving into a "pear-shaped"
labour market, with a small labour aristocracy at the top and a swelling
group of "non-standard" employees at the bottom. By the mid-to-late
1980s, Canada's major cities were seeing record sales of luxury automo-
biles and record lineups at food banks.[2] The "shrinking middle" raised the

prospect of Canadian society becoming increasingly shaped along the lines of the archetypal Latin American state, with concentrated wealth plunked down immediately alongside glaring poverty.

The shrinking of job openings at the middle level was an immediate concern for labour, because union dues are usually paid from a percentage of wages. For example, the Steelworker members who lost their jobs when Brian Mulroney closed down the Schefferville mine in Quebec in 1982 had earned double the wages of the industrial security guards who took their place in the union. Hence they had paid double the union dues. When Inco cut back on its operations in Sudbury during the early 1980s, the miners who lost their jobs and still wanted to stay on in the city had to move into work at hotels or hardware stores or

Fred Pomeroy, founding president of the CWC, *and now president of the* CEP.

non-union construction firms, with a sharp decline of income – if they could get jobs at all. The remaining (unionized) Inco miners were increasingly isolated at the top of the region's industrial wage scale, while their former colleagues were massed at the bottom.

The Premier's Council that Fred Pomeroy was involved in was a sign of the times. Liberal premier David Peterson had established it in the mid-1980s to seek more "concertation" in economic planning – more involvement particularly by business and labour in the economic policies of the provincial government – as part of a broad effort to reposition Ontario in a shifting global economy. On the Council Fred and two other union representatives faced a couple of dozen leaders from business, education, and government.

In the sphere of worker education the key tension between labour and business was between labour's conception of training as a right of citizenship and business's emphasis on labour-market needs. As he read into the wee hours of the morning Fred Pomeroy found that the draft report emphasized to a dismaying degree the business side, especially the concerns that were dominating government policy discussions of job training: competitiveness and skill shortages. Fred saw the assumptions behind the text as technocratic and elitist, and became increasingly upset.

For labour the problem was that, in training as elsewhere, "them what has, gets." One study found that participation in adult education programs was extremely inequitable. In 1988 only 5 per cent of elementary school drop-outs took an adult education course, but nearly half of all university graduates were enrolled in some form of further education.[3] Even within unionized workplaces, the bulk of training went to young, able-bodied white men with postsecondary certificates. The inequalities of wealth and social power in the society at large were reproduced in the workplace, and the conservative push to privatize and build a system around the principles of competitiveness would not help the situation.

On the morning after he stayed up reading the draft report, Fred Pomeroy arrived sleep-deprived, but informed, at the downtown Toronto hotel for the Premier's Council meeting. He told the gathering, dominated by corporate and government people, that from labour's point of view the ideas outlined in the report were "totally unacceptable." He said that if the approach wasn't changed the three union members would have to leave the Council.

To Fred's horror, Premier Peterson turned the tables, coolly suggesting that the government would fund "you labour people" to rewrite the report.

Fred pondered a bit as he walked across College Street to the union building. When he got there he dropped into my office. That fall he had called on me a couple of times to prepare or present material on issues of economic renewal and technological change, stuff needed to support his participation on the Council. He told me about the meeting and the problems with the report and said dryly: "Look, I don't want you to misunderstand, I think you should have Christmas Day off. But rewrite the report. The future of civilization hangs in the balance." I got the impression that the project was to be given priority.

Joining me on the task were two other staff representatives – John O'Grady, the research director of the Ontario Federation of Labour, and Hugh Mackenzie of the Steelworkers – selected by the other two labour leaders on the Council. We assembled a think tank to work with the labour movement on this policy issue, because we felt we couldn't keep up with the speed and intricacy of changes on our own.

At this time both training users and providers were experiencing a mounting dissatisfaction with the existing relationships around training. For many individual learners, the system of training opportunities had become too complex and too uncertain in its link to meaningful and well-compensated jobs in an increasingly volatile labour market. Employers were complaining that the system was not satisfying their needs for a flexible, motivated workforce capable of sustaining the "competitive advantage" that was seen as crucial to corporate survival. For labour, the system was elitist, fragmented, and filled with dead ends. Social action advocates had a completely different fix on things: they thought it was time to use training to address systemic barriers of exclusion and marginalization in the workplace.

A system driven largely by government and established training providers was under pressure to change.

Our group worked through the recommendations in the business-oriented draft and changed them one by one. The counterreport we produced dealt comprehensively with training, adjustment, and education. In the education section, which I worked on, we affirmed the central role of the public school system in promoting equality of education, both in opportunity and outcome. This meant resisting conservative proposals for privatizing education. We also affirmed the role of education in personal development rather than limiting it to certain employment skills. We wanted the Premier's Council to support the movement away from streamed education, to ensure that working-class children would have access to success in the schools and not be shunted into "dead end" programs.

We developed similar guidelines for job training and adjustment and by early March had completed a draft that the union representatives on the Council fully supported. At that point we thought our job was done. We expected the business representatives to reject the guidelines and walk away from the table. That would neatly end labour's involvement in what was a tricky collaboration. From our point of view that would be

99

okay; it would allow the labour movement to print our version as a counterreport, and we could use that version to help critique the expected establishment report.

That's when we got the second surprise. The business representatives on the Council said, "Okay, we'll bargain." With that began a series of drafting meetings lasting for three months to produce a compromise text we could all live with. As the bargaining over policy continued, we briefed Opposition Leader Bob Rae's office and the Ontario NDP caucus. It took a major commitment of staff time over several months to develop and defend our perspective.

The final document, *People and Skills in the New Global Economy*, released on July 25, 1990, proposed the establishment of an Ontario Training and Adjustment Board to co-ordinate public and private sector initiatives. There was to be a strong union voice at all levels of the board's work.

■ ■ ■ ■

For years labour leaders had been pressing to gain a more substantial role in shaping the country's economic future. Many felt that the only way to protect a high-wage workforce was through high productivity and high skill, through building the capacity for rapid and high-quality output. But until the late 1980s the labour movement was given short shrift in a policy climate dominated by neoconservatism.

The balance shifted, however slightly and particularly in Ontario, with the efforts of Peterson's Liberals to court the labour vote. Meanwhile, from 1987 to 1990, Ontario's electrical and electronics industry, including both business and labour, launched the Sectoral Skills Council (SSC). The SSC and the Canadian Steel Trade and Employment Council in the steel industry became the points of reference for sectoral labour-market and training policy. These bodies brought employers and unions together outside the collective bargaining context to seek common ground in the midst of massive economic restructuring. Their supporters argued that competitors could co-operate in sustaining a whole industry and that business and labour in a particular industry were more accurately attuned to training needs than were the government officials and education providers currently in charge.

The opening chapter of the Premier's Council report noted that while Sweden, West Germany, and Japan differed in many respects, all of them offered more adjustment and training support to workers than Canada did, a factor that empowered employees in those countries to face the future with some confidence. The report stated: "The proliferation of programs and overlapping jurisdictional responsibilities [in Ontario] generates confusion, not effective choice. . . . Trying to get at government training programs is sometimes like trying to shop at a supermarket whose location is undisclosed and whose prices are kept secret."

When a majority NDP government was elected in Ontario in September 1990, followed by similar victories in Saskatchewan and British Columbia, a significant political bloc emerged to reshape labour-market policies across the country.[4] The Premier's Council became a key policy forum within the NDP administration in Ontario, for instance, and Fred Pomeroy remained an active member. (Interestingly, the Premier's Council was one of the first agencies abolished by Ontario's Conservative government after its electoral victory in June 1995.)

The context of union representation on training issues was new for people accustomed to collective bargaining: the new structures being set up were mostly sectoral, bipartite, and devolved. They were *sectoral* because they were based on economic sectors such as electrical manufacturing, auto parts, and steel-making – covering both non-union and unionized workplaces and possibly requiring several unions as well as competing employers to work together. They were *bipartite* because business and labour had a joint role: both had equal representation and sole voting authority. This meant that a failure to compromise could deadlock the whole venture. They were *devolved* because governments passed real authority over real money to the new bodies, rather than treating them as advisory or consultative.

Union reps on these councils, then, had to consider training needs for a whole sector, not just an individual workplace. They had to compromise, and they had to allocate relatively large budgets. Since 1988 I have sat with the other five union reps on the Sectoral Skills Council, set up to bring employers and unions in the electrical and electronic sector together to plan jointly for the future "human resource" needs of the industry. From the beginning it seemed that we were constantly learning like mad.

Companies were more willing to include labour in planning around issues of training than on investment in technological design. As a result, training became the focus for a broader debate among unions over the potential and limits of co-operative ventures with management. Some unions in electrical and electronic manufacturing were hesitant about participating in the Sectoral Skills Council, and in mid-1989 the Canadian Auto Workers withdrew from the process. (They rejoined it in 1994.) In turn, some employers believed that labour had little to contribute to the training process, especially when many of the plants in the particular sector were not unionized.

As labour began asserting its role in shaping wealth creation as well as wealth distribution, some union leaders began to seek the legitimacy in economic life that Canadians accord to the "loyal opposition" in political life. Labour leaders speaking out about the harmful trends of the time increasingly addressed the business community as a whole, rather than individual employers. They began calling for "social bargaining" based on the causes and effects of the current economic restructuring.

For me, social bargaining became an integral part of the work of the new Sectoral Skills Council. The term implied "a process for reconciling diverse interests," a process that sat somewhere between the consensual and adversarial styles of operation, an expansion of the range of co-operative activity. In the case of the Sectoral Skills Council, the process became one of social bargaining rather than collective bargaining because of who was involved and what was being addressed.

The actors (or, as some prefer, "social partners") are business, labour, government, and educators. Within each of these four actors, there is much diversity. A narrow, workplace-based collective bargaining model cannot encompass this range of participants, nor can it take in the scope of SSC activities. Further, the issues of learning that are central to the SSC cannot all be quantified and spelled out in the binding contract language of collective bargaining.

■ ■ ■ ■

With the restructuring of Canada's economy, the labour movement required changed attitudes, and union educators gained new responsibilities. Labour representatives needed training and coaching to participate in structures like the Sectoral Skills Council, especially if those structures were not to be controlled entirely from the top. Shared responsibility raised problems of co-optation, and union representatives needed time to shift their emotional stance without abandoning their identity. Unions tended to work through these issues more in conferences and meetings than in formal courses, but sometimes the education staff played a direct role – providing background documents, films, speakers, and on occasion drafting policy proposals.

The process of adaptation created a new strain on people like me, go-betweens between the membership and the leadership. In most of the policy discussions that the leaders participated in, feelings were muted. The national union leaders would gradually become impatient with the "petty" expressions of pain that permeated local union discussions. The pressures of public opinion and the disciplines of public social bargaining inclined them to anaesthetize the pain, to adopt a more "responsible" approach, which in turn imposed a new set of risks for the union educator in the "politics of levels" that always operate in labour. The job of building workers' confidence, skill, and knowledge extends into a passionate commitment that the voices of workers be heard. But the pain of the members and the anaesthesia of the leaders at times create strains for those who talk to both.

The business establishment, along with the government, asked labour to join the discussions within these new institutions because of the particular economic climate of the 1980s, the dramatic restructuring of workplace conditions, and the wholesale dumping of workers from jobs. At the same time labour exacted a price for its participation: a shift on the part of business not only on the specific issues but also in recognizing labour as a credible and thoughtful force in economic and training policy.

At an international policy conference on "Technology and the Global Economy" held in Montreal in 1991, Fred Pomeroy told an elite gathering, "The exclusive managerial right to design and re-organize work has to be set aside." Under certain conditions, unions would co-operate to enhance productivity in the workplace. There had already been some successes:

> Our steady pressure has resulted in factoring in human needs at telephone companies across Canada. In Manitoba, management and the union have set up joint work design teams, which removed individual electronic monitoring, allowed operators unlimited trades in scheduling, addressed the causes of electric shocks and other physical hazards. Here the empowerment of workers and increased productivity have gone hand in hand, to the benefit of all.

Unions, Fred said, "should not be reactive about employment security for workers." Instead, "In a volatile, globalized economy, we should take the offensive, creating the conditions for skilled, interesting, dignified and well-paid employment" – even if this meant "taking criticism" or "admitting mistakes and starting all over again." He added, "But I believe the status quo is riskier in the long run than the innovations we propose."[5] Central to these innovations were structures like the Sectoral Skills Council.

With this social bargaining it seemed that unions were finally getting members' needs for training met. In the Sectoral Skills Council, for example, we won a commitment that training would only be funded if it provided portable skills in an equitable way, in addition to existing training activities. And proposals from unionized workplaces required the signature of a union rep to be approved.

In addition to the SSC work I became a member of the Ontario Federation of Labour's Training Subcommittee, working to develop, alongside other unions, a co-ordinated policy and strategy on training issues. At the same time I co-ordinated a team of worker-researchers in assessing the training needs of our CWC members in the Industrial Sector. In the course of this work, I became actively aware of the employer focus on "competitiveness" and of the need to develop a worker-driven agenda. And I remembered the advice Bert Munro had given to me in my early days at the Steelworkers, about starting "to quack" if I flew too much with the ducks. We had to keep in mind other imperatives, always.

What we wanted to avoid was "competency-based" training – training as defined by management. Its aim was to "train" workers to "perform" separate, unrelated tasks. It would lead to fragmented, rigid jobs and discourage critical, creative thinking by workers – in the process undermining any union power in the workplace. "Worker-driven training," on the contrary, would aim at maximizing the amount of control in the hands of the workers by deepening, not fragmenting, their understanding of the workplace processes. It would be defined by workers and encourage them to exercise, sharpen, and act on their judgements. The training would be about more than boosting productivity and profits. As one report put it, "Our aim is to build meaningful and secure futures for ourselves and our communities."[6]

The training issue, I thought, was one that could increase union presence in the workplace, and I took this position in union meetings and at conferences. Traditional unionism, centring on the grievance procedure between rounds of collective bargaining, had mostly touched the minority who had personal disputes with management. Through health and safety, we had begun knitting unionism into the lives of the other three-quarters of our members – people who more or less ignored the union once a contract was settled. Training could be another channel for involving and representing a broad range of members in the daily life of the union. In the long term this channel might complement membership education courses.

I thought we should gradually shift the balance towards training that was broad rather than narrowly limited to one task or job – so that workers could gain the ability to take on a variety of tasks in the future;

towards worker-driven training, rather than competency-based; and towards choice by the learner rather than flexibility for the employer. In this respect, training was like tech change: a general union concern that had not been successfully addressed in collective bargaining.[7]

THE LEVELS OF SOCIAL BARGAINING

For unions, the new labour-management structures that emerged to deal with training across the country posed issues of strategy at five levels: the workplace, the sector, the local community, the province, and Canada-wide.

In the workplace we have seen examples of management losing patience with power-sharing and trying to push the union right out of decision-making. Yet gradually local managers recognized that learning cannot be coerced and that employees can most readily improve their job skills – and thus benefit the company – by voluntarily working through their union.

The manufacturing plants represented by CWC had a particularly tough time dealing with employers on the established one by one basis. If local unions and local management were to reach constructive agreements, they needed technical support and clout with government funders and educational providers as well as with head offices in other countries. This could best be achieved by linking arms with other firms in the same economic sector. That's why we began working at the second level, the sector.

At the sectoral level employers were acutely aware that most of their future employees were already in the workplace, and that they should train those workers rather than wait for youth or immigrants to replace them. It was also at this level that unions in turn had to recognize the intensity of the employers' "free rider" problem. When we convinced a single employer to train our members, a neighbouring employer could raid the resulting skilled workers by offering slightly higher wages. The employer's investment would wind up benefiting the competitors.

In the end, six business and six labour representatives in the Sectoral Skills Council hammered out a framework agreement on training policy and invited workplaces to opt into it. We adopted three guidelines for funding each training proposal generated in the workplace: the key words were incremental, portable, and equitable. *Incremental* meant that the training must involve programs not already offered by the company. *Portable* meant that it must develop capacities not specific to the particular workplace. (If workers got dumped they would have some educational capital to take along to their next job.) *Equitable* meant that everyone in a workplace would have a recognized entitlement to learn. Business and labour agreed that if a training initiative was not incremental, portable, and equitable, it should not get supported by the fund.

At the third level, the local community, the dynamics were significantly different. On the workplace and sectoral levels, only management and labour are directly involved. But in the community, both business and labour have to deal more extensively with government and address the issues raised, for instance, by equity advocates. As the process evolved, the parties had to deal with completely unfamiliar learning needs, like those of Francophone Ontarians or agricultural producers. For example, the overwhelmingly anglo and urban leaders of business and labour were being told that 18 to 25 per cent of jobs in Ontario were directly related to agriculture: "If we don't have primary producers, we don't have these jobs. You can argue all you like about the wonders of computers, but try to eat a hard disk."[8]

The fourth main level of social bargaining has been provincial. In Ontario particularly, the Ontario Training and Adjustment Board (OTAB) was set up to allocate federal and provincial funds, with elaborate participatory structures in which labour and business played the key role. The proposal for OTAB, first advanced under the Liberal government, was developed further after the election of the NDP in 1990. In the course of consultation meetings, the uneven power relations among labour-market partners became increasingly apparent. Consultation with stakeholders at a province-wide level led to release of a discussion paper on a revised OTAB structure in November 1991.

Steering committees from each "labour-market partner" then nominated participants for a travelling panel that would go out and seek input from communities across the province on how the emerging structures for training could best be anchored locally. This panel was to work from a discussion document and report back on community response. The OFL named Erna Post of the Public Service Alliance of Canada and myself to this panel. My own involvement also included participation in the labour reference group that dealt with the establishment of the OTAB.

At times the gulf in perceptions and priorities between labour and business was enormous, and the needs on both sides pressing. By the end of Ontario's NDP government, in 1995, the OTAB had just begun establishment of Local Boards, more than four years behind schedule.[9]

The fifth level of social bargaining is Canada-wide, and here the Canadian Labour Force Development Board has played a role. While the Board's advisory status and the shifting of responsibilities for training to the provinces as part of a new Canadian constitution have both affected its viability, the Board's influence in setting the terms of debate around training has been considerable.

Since the Board was established, with Gérard Docquier as co-chair and Fred Pomeroy as a labour representative, I have had continuing contact with that process – which proved a good occasion to rebuild my personal relationship with Gérard Docquier, a relationship that was so important to me in the early 1980s and so damaged by the political rift between us in the "civil war time" of 1985. I found our collaboration growing once again throughout the Local Board consultation process in the spring of 1992, as well as in other occasions like a Conference Board of Canada conference that we worked on together. The reconciliation was capped by my attendance at a testimonial dinner for Gérard in June 1992.

As unions begin to co-ordinate action among these five levels, we will need to make careful preparations and pay particular attention to building our internal capacities. Gradually, through the experience of participation and through internal reflection in the membership education program, labour can develop its strengths and renew its vision in this new terrain.

As the Ontario Federation of Labour guidelines put it, "Training programs must be open to all, not just the youngest or fittest members of the workforce. Training must become a vehicle for correcting the discrimination that women, visible minorities, native people and the disabled have had to contend with in both the educational system and the workplace." The workers themselves should identify their skills needs, rather than having employers or consultants restrict those needs to "narrowly-defined performance factors."

In addition, according to the OFL, "Skills training must enable workers to have more control over their jobs. In this way the training experience becomes a genuinely empowering one – individually and collectively. . . . Skills training must incorporate the practices of good adult education, starting with an understanding of what participants already know and what they want to know. It must respect the many abilities people bring to training, and encourage questioning, discussion and participation."

Proper skills training would also help employees work more safely. It would help them learn about their individual and collective rights. Skills training, the OFL guidelines state, "must equip the participant to put that knowledge and experience into action." It could also help companies develop better job design as well as "technology that enhances the skills of workers."[10]

This OFL perspective, widely understood and supported throughout the union movement, did not emerge easily. And it was not easily accepted by the other participants in the training policy process. But it was clear, progressive, and consistent with the values of the union culture. The OFL guidelines have since become the basis of discussion in other provinces and within affiliated unions. They provide a clear example of how policy work can feed back into the life of the labour movement, both guiding and inspiring action at the grassroots level.

By early 1992, while I was still working on my assignments in policy, I became aware that Fred Pomeroy's focus had moved back to the workings of the CWC itself. In particular, he had begun approaching other unions to join forces, "to merge, not to submerge," as he put it. He had less and less patience for the needs and voices of public "stakeholders" and increasing interest in the constitutional and financial implications of linking up the CWC with other unions. Indeed, a series of discussions with leaders of the Energy and Chemical Workers Union (ECWU) and the Canadian Paperworkers Union (CPU) led to a proposal to create a new, large private-sector union.

These three Canadian unions, of roughly equal size, became the core of a new force in labour, the CEP, founded on November 28, 1992. While I have remained involved in policy discussions, my work priority since then has returned to the member education that brought me into the labour movement in the first place.

EIGHT

MERGER TIME

■ ■ ■ ■

Nothing has been lost if we hold onto our courage, by proclaiming that
everything has been lost and we are ready to start all over again.

— Julio Cortazar

The message on my voice mail was clear enough: "D'Arcy, I want to bring
together the people who have been doing education in all parts of the
union. Let me know if you *can't* make it to a meeting at the national office
in Ottawa on January 25."

It was the first time I had heard directly from Don Holder, president of
my newly merged union, the Communications, Energy and Paperworkers
Union of Canada (CEP). The actual merger convention, bringing together
unions from three sectors – communications/ electrical, energy/ chemical
and pulp/ paper – had taken place when I was on a study leave in November 1992. I had met Don Holder briefly during the merger negotiations,
but in the few months since returning from my leave I had never had
occasion to talk with him.

It didn't take a rocket scientist to know that this was less an invitation
than a command performance. I had already worked on an introductory
steward manual for the merged union and forwarded a draft of it to Trish
Blackstaffe, an old friend who was now one of Don Holder's assistants. I
called her on the phone to find out something about the upcoming meeting, but she gave me little detail except to say that it was the first chance
for people to hear from each other about the union's education programs

in different regions and sectors. The day before the meeting with Holder I had a planning session in Toronto with two Ontario staff from the paper sector to trade ideas on what our region might try to get out of the Ottawa meeting.

The next morning a dozen or so people were seated in the national office boardroom in downtown Ottawa. Don Holder asked us each to state our name and current assignments. Then he said, "Before turning the meeting over to D'Arcy, I want to emphasize that it is time to merge our efforts in the educational field. For all of you, this is now top priority." He pointed to a copy of my draft steward manual and said it was the starting point of discussion. Then he gestured to me to take over the chair. Realizing that this was no time to be shy, I started off on the roles of the steward – to inform, defend, and build unity among members.

Things seemed to go well enough, and five hours later the meeting wound up after producing the outline of a work plan for the coming months. We had just scheduled a follow-up meeting when someone thought to ask, "Okay, but what do I call this group?" Don Holder replied, "This is the CEP National Education Committee. Your work will be a centrepiece of the November convention."

The rest of us took this in – some people stopped to scribble the name in their notebooks – and then we all began packing up our assorted papers to head back home. My mind strayed back to my first day on the job at the Steelworkers, to my first exposure to the peculiar chemistry of union life: something that seemed both haphazard and powerful. But here and now, if there were loose ends there was no doubt about the president's overall direction. He said I would be interim co-ordinator of the group's work, and that I and others were to reschedule any obligations that conflicted with getting the job done. We needed to produce a three-day course manual with appropriate videos, activities, and readings for new stewards, then test it all and prepare staff to teach the course. Once this was under way, we would move on to working with experienced stewards, then new local officers, and so forth through the organization.

Afterwards Don congratulated me on how I had handled the meeting and made a commitment to provide the budget and staff support necessary to get things going. I reminded him that I wasn't able to move to Ottawa, so my co-ordination role would have to be an interim one until an education director could be hired for the national office. Soon after that I took a taxi to the airport, my mind in a bit of a whirl.

In the departure lounge of the Ottawa airport I joined three union reps who were having a beer. One of them had been at the planning session with me the day before. He remarked that I had done a "smooth" job of chairing. I shrugged, saying it was the best I could do without previous notice. A little sceptically, he asked if I had planned the agenda ahead of time with Don Holder. One of the others stepped in then: "Actually, I walked into the office with Don this morning. He told me there was no set agenda, that this was a chance to look at how we could start working together. When we came in D'Arcy was on the phone in the waiting room. Don pointed to him and asked me who he was."

Luckily for me, this convinced the other rep that Don and I hadn't set up the meeting together. It turned out that he thought I had been "less than frank" with him in our earlier conversations and that he had been feeling tricked all through the meeting that day, especial-

Trish Blackstaffe, assistant to the president of CEP.

ly because the discussion had moved along so well. He had become suspicious that there had been a pre-set national agenda, and that our regional planning meeting the previous day had been a sham. He paused, smiled, and said, "Let me buy you a beer. You earned it."

Again, here was a display of that delicate thread of trust inside the union. It had been tested and was now strengthened. The rep would become an important ally in our work to develop a unified education program for the CEP.

After that first day I entered eight months of intense production. With writer Bev Burke and video producer Don Bouzek, I pulled together the study materials for a new "Steward I" course. With staff Nicole Brulé, Trish Blackstaffe, and Cathy Hallessey, I designed and tested the bilingual kits that participants would need. By the time education director Bob Hatfield was hired in September, the education ball was rolling under the slogan "Collective Effective Participation . . . CEP." Little tests of trust continued to take place over these months amongst us all, amidst a growing

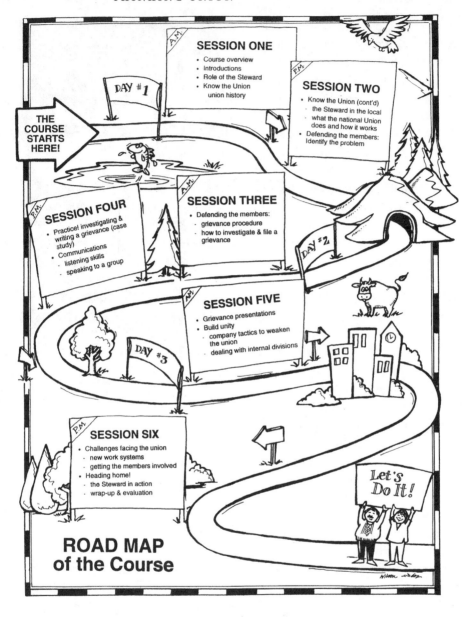

ROAD MAP of the Course

The road map for the three-day Steward I course,
developed for CEP by Bev Burke.

sense of pleasure and accomplishment. For me personally, this marked the third time I would work to rebuild a member education program from the ground up.

COLLECTIVE EFFECTIVE PARTICIPATION: FRAMEWORKS

Sometimes it seems to me as if certain core elements in the organizational package developed in the Steelworkers' "back to the locals" program have never gone away. The union education work I have done ever since has involved many of the same functions: increasing and updating courses for stewards, enabling union activists to teach courses, building up financial support for education, making course locations and scheduling more accessible, and co-ordinating courses.

These are largely procedural matters, essentially tactics. They are important enough in themselves, but a complete educational strategy needs to go deeper. Certainly, workers are not seeking "neutral" education when they come to a union course. They want support and shared risk. They call on the union educator to define a social and ethical ground, to take a stand on issues. This is different than in the formal education system, where many adult educators are convinced that "professionalism" requires a withdrawal from the learning process at the point when people begin to test their knowledge and feelings in action. Union education is different because it essentially begins, like all union work, from questions of power. After all, the labour movement's purpose is to win more power for workers. Education should help to renew and democratize union structures and to equip worker representatives for a broad range of challenges and responsibilities.

In an attempt to focus this strategy more explicitly, I have put increasing effort into specifying who is involved in the learning and what objectives I am actually pursuing – that is, why I am doing the teaching in the first place. For the "who," I think in terms of *participants*, *educators*, and *sponsors*. For the objectives, the "why," I think in terms of *knowing*, *feeling*, and *doing*.

THE WHO IN THE LEARNING

I have come to believe that the educator's bias should be that of a "radical democrat," constantly seeking to develop and draw upon insights from the rank and file and providing options and challenges to the leadership.

The elected union leader's bias needs to be "strategic negotiator," judging the times when unity is required for effectiveness with employers and governments, and exercising political discipline at those points.

In trade union education, the *participants* are active in the union culture, often people committed to particular alliances and political positions in the organizational life of the movement. This means that to be effective union education must necessarily focus on the wider web of social identities, on the world inhabited by working-class learners, a world filled with contradictions and inequities.[1] It must focus on changing power relations.

Without this deep commitment to change, in the course as well as in the world outside, education becomes, according to Paulo Freire, "an act of depositing, in which the students are the depositories and the teacher is the depositor. Instead of communicating, the teacher issues communiques and makes deposits which the students patiently receive, memorize, and repeat."[2] In union education, education staff and local union course leaders each bring particular perspectives to the image of the educator. Some of us are identified with particular political currents within the labour movement – perhaps with a particular union leader, a women's caucus, or an international solidarity network. Our sympathies, friendships, and incomes are intimately tied to the political fate of that current, and some activists move through the educator role as a stepping stone to some other level of leadership. To locate educators is a social and political exercise.

In a union the *sponsor* is the elected leadership, which means that union education has to take into account the tensions in the union structure itself. Although self-directed learning among members can occur independently of the political and economic conditions of the union, acute internal rivalries or dropping dues income can change the encounter of participant with educator. To be fully effective, educational leadership should remain distinct from political leadership, since both are required for a healthy and effective social movement. Good educational leadership has a dual role to play: not only contributing to learning among the members, but also working to keep the political leadership – the sponsors – open to new learning from participants.

The energy of union education, then, is in the interaction among these three parties, and the art of the democratic educator is in getting the balance right. I am acutely conscious that participants' learning is necessarily in the participants' own hands, and that my role as educator is to create the best possible conditions for that learning: by negotiating conditions with the union as sponsor, by developing my craft, and by sharing power with the participants.

114

The adults attending a trade union course are in a strong position to contribute what they know to a shared venture. They are an empowered and activist group within the working class. They have chosen to come, and they have the financial and political support of co-workers in attending. The political task of the union educator is to weaken, carefully and skilfully, the hold of dominant ideas on participants in union courses, and to strengthen the emerging good sense as part of the equipment of an increasingly confident social movement. In the process educators do "the learning" alongside the students/ participants.

This is not to say that I have not been discouraged about the prospects for success in this work from time to time. At one such time, in 1987, I wrote and circulated a short poem, "Educator's Gamble." The last two verses went:

> The court jesters
> and snake oil salesmen
> of the silicon age
> are on the loose.
> Social vandals are looting
> our lottery of dreams unborn.

> Is this game stacked?
> Is it the only game in town?
> It's time for us
> to breathe deeply,
> think twice,
> then bet with all our heart.

A consistently democratic and problem-posing union education can tap wisdom and channel anger in ways that contribute to genuine social transformation. But the recurring, rewarding experience of personal growth, challenge, and excitement in interaction with street-smart workers is what has sustained me day by day.

For radical educators, the challenge is to maximize the involvement of participants in setting the direction and pace of the course. This means doing within the union culture what Freire and other popular educators have been doing amidst the intricacies of Latin American society – identifying and working from *generative themes*. This in turn means first testing the waters for common experiences that are important to participants' everyday lives – whether they are bingo games or grievances or alcoholism. Then we need to discuss the patterns in experience through conscious and critical dialogue. This implies direct contact with groups of learners, moving perceptions from naive to critical understanding, from common sense to good sense. And the test of learning is in action, transformative action, a direct challenge to existing power relations.

THE WHY OF UNION EDUCATION

Keeping in mind the specifics of the participants, educators, and sponsors, a union educator can set particular objectives for a course, a series of courses, or a program in general. These objectives should articulate the knowing, feeling, and doing expected of participants at the end. Passing on "information" is only one level of the educational encounter, and dealing with various levels of emotion and skill requires equal if not greater attention.

Knowing refers to the critical awareness that we as educators feel the participants need to have by the end of the course. *Feeling* refers to the emotional stance of participants towards the course, the issue, and the union. And *doing* means developing the skills for winning the hearts and minds of our members.

Here, for instance, are the objectives for a three-day course in 1994, worked out with local union officers of a small regional phone company in northern Ontario:

KNOW . . .
that together CEP and the company have formulated a job security statement;
that Northern Telephone Limited is not the only company in the world doing this;
that the union's goal is the same as before . . . to inform, protect and defend our members.

FEEL . . .
that members have pride in their work and more job satisfaction;
that they have involvement in decision making, a voice at Northern Telephone Limited;
that their union is holding the company responsible in making these changes.

116

DO . . .
take ownership of the change;
hold the company responsible for effecting the full set of changes, not
picking those convenient at the moment;
monitor the changes and inform the union executive, to ensure equality and fairness for all.

We used these goals for a members' briefing in the company's home base
of Timmins, Ontario, in a workplace that was undergoing heavy restructuring. The course provided an opportunity to build union presence in the
workplace and to apply union principles creatively to new conditions on
the job.

Still, there are many obstacles to a full balance of knowing, feeling, and
doing in union education. Indeed, many of the "communications difficulties" experienced by educators in unions can be traced to an imbalance of
the three. Each of them can be distorted when cut off from the others.

A first approach, heavy on knowing, is "research-driven." Its central
commitment is to the content of a social issue – perhaps racism, sexism, or
class bias. Energy and skill go into studying the particular matter and confronting people with findings. The participants' and sponsors' reaction to
this stance is often to plead overload, which in turn can justify paralysis.
One time in a workshop on technology, when I erred on this side, a participant commented, "I came looking for a glass of water, and found I was
dealing with a fire hydrant." I had been aiming at collective clarity, but my
effect was to overwhelm this particular learner and alienate him from the
issue.

The second approach, heavy on the affective level, is "feeling-driven."
Its central commitment is to group process and psychic empowerment.
Here the educator's energy and skill go into listening and shepherding the
group towards an intuitive consensus based on information already present among the participants. If participants come seeking a glass of water
in this case, they might instead get a stream of consciousness.

The third approach, with a heavy emphasis on the skills to be developed by participants, is "action-driven." It seeks a public outcome, whatever the price. Instead of a glass of water they get a hose and are told to
put out the fire. In union life the test of success for education is often the
number of participants who later engage in voluntary action on the issues
raised. This instrumental approach to education is analogous to those who
assess the value of a theatre production by computing the number of
"bums on seats."

None of these approaches can be effective in isolation. A responsible educational strategy means working in three dimensions at once – developing a solid grounding in the content of issues; charting the emotional snakes and ladders along the route; and developing an internal compass that guides towards effective individual and collective action.

WORKPLACE REORGANIZATION

These frameworks, then, have guided my work in a large, merged private-sector union. They require me to think twice about what I am doing, rather than to work from habit, to reflect on who is involved, and to balance my objectives.

This work, because it is not socially or politically neutral, takes a stand, and encourages others to do the same. I aim, as my daughter Nyranne said, to "teach workers how to talk back."

The primary place in which union activists need to talk back is the workplace. Whether the labour leadership becomes engaged in social bargaining, or labour radicals are reaching out to social coalitions, their claim to represent workers' interests still rests in the workplace. Most members get their direct experience of the union in relation to workplace issues. Their central choice is whether to approach the employer in a spirit of intelligent co-operation, of reluctant obedience, or of militant resistance.

This choice first became clear for me during a course in Alberta, when one of our members, who worked as an airport ticket agent, told us a workplace story. The month before he had received a circular from the accounting department noting that a lot of pens were being carried off by passengers from the ticket agent desks. The memo tersely stated: "There will only be four pens issued per shift." The ticket agents in that airport got a friend in maintenance to drill a little hole in their desks and chain the pens down. This was awkward for the customer and slowed down the job of ticketing, but the agents ran through less than four pens per shift, which presumably made the accounting department happy, at least until the slowdown of business began to show.

Ticket agents at another airport got the same directive but responded less wholeheartedly. Passengers accidentally continued to pick up pens, and at most booths after about an hour and a half of the first shift the fourth pen was gone. When that happened the next passenger who tried to borrow a pen to sign a ticket was told, "I'm sorry, we only have four pens per shift." Then the ticket agent would step out helpfully from behind the counter and walk down the line of waiting passengers to find one willing to lend a pen. Halfway through the shift the departure lounge was in chaos; by the end of the shift, the directive had been rescinded. The passive resistance of staff in that second airport – their reluctant obedience – had achieved quick results.

Stories like this abound in union life. They show how workers directly get back at arrogant and arbitrary treatment, by following to the letter an instruction that they know will be self-defeating. In a Sudbury mine one time workers fully assembled a new Swedish drilling machine under the over-attentive eye of a young engineer, knowing that it was being pointed in the wrong direction in a narrow drift. In a Toronto warehouse, phone company employees let a manager flourish his requisition authority by purchasing cupboards a foot too short to hold the items to be stored there.

For employers, the intelligent co-operation of employees can save money, and reluctant obedience can be expensive. The companies' recognition of this is at the heart of their new efforts to focus the hearts and minds of employees on "productivity" through management-driven schemes such as "employee empowerment," "total quality management," and "high commitment systems."[3] These efforts create a new opportunity, and a new set of challenges, for the labour movement. Union policy initiatives in this area are often referred to as "workplace reorganization." My own connection with this has been primarily in the telecommunications sector, particularly with the giant Bell Canada and the small Northern Telephone, and I have found that effectively designing and conducting education for workers that deals with these new concerns require a level of power-sharing and disclosure on the part of companies that few devotees of "re-engineering" are prepared to undertake.

In anticipating change, the CEP has sought to gain more than a rubber stamp on management initiatives. The union articulated its terms for involvement at a "New Directions" conference held in 1994. At Shell Sarnia, Saskatchewan Chemicals, Manitoba Telephone Limited, Phillips Cables, and New Brunswick Telephone, union bargaining committees have wrestled with this challenge. In the particular conditions of their workplaces, they have argued that ongoing improvements in quality, productivity, and innovation should flow from the full, creative involvement of employees and their union in the decision-making process.

This involved drafting guidelines and then discussing and revising them in meetings with union officers and bargaining committees and assisting in the presentation of the ideas to employers. It also required defending this perspective against those in the labour movement who saw it as "collaboration" with employers, which would inevitably wind up, like my experience at Dominion Stores in Windsor, by hurting the members. Our immediate goal was to gain a share of power and responsibility for designing the workplace, including the selection, content, and methods of training and retraining our members. We had four long-term goals for joint workplace reorganization:

- ensuring employment security and expanding employment opportunities.
- maintaining a high and rising standard of living.
- providing a high degree of equity and fairness for all employees, including the opportunity to take advantage of new technologies, work processes, and techniques that are needed to advance their careers.
- giving employees more input into workplace decisions and greater control over their work, with concurrent reductions in unhealthy forms of stress and improvements in employment satisfaction that result from job enrichment.

In 1993 Northern Telephone management invited union representative John Edwards to help bring his union into a partnership that would be "customer-driven." Obviously struck by a certain amount of mixed feelings about this venture, Edwards wrote to local activists:

As unionists, we have always struggled for a voice. If we have asked for nothing else, we have asked to be heard, to be a part of the process.

Well, the door appears to be open right now at Northern Telephone Limited. Are we afraid to enter? Are we afraid the door will close and trap us inside? What is our obligation?

We should do more than just barge in and speak our minds. We should first remove the wall that holds the door in place. Only then can we guarantee that never again will the door be closed, trapping us on either side.[4]

The symbol of walls has echoes for each of us . . . from Jericho to Berlin to Pink Floyd and Shirley Valentine. Canadian unions aren't currently well equipped or experienced in taking down such walls. We're more comfortable pounding on doors. Even if we don't accomplish anything, union activists are secure in that ritual. We know what we're doing, as do the members and the managers. Why change?

Edwards's statement invites us to look past the door of arbitrary management practices to the frame and structure that gives those practices legal and cultural support. The problem, he suggests, isn't the door but the wall. Standing back to take in the full dimensions of the wall is our first step. Then we have to gain a critical perspective on our traditional way of thinking about management.

THE EDUCATION SKIT, AND MORE

In late November 1994, the new CEP had its first constitutional convention following the merger. "Education" had an hour-long slot on the morning of the last day and, as a change of pace after three days of reports, speeches, and debates, Bob Hatfield devised what would become known as the "education skit." After a display of coloured lights dancing around the ceiling, and then a short introduction by Bob, four "historical workers" appeared at the audience microphones and began speaking about what learning was like in their times and places: a printer from the 1870s, a phone operator from 1919, a refinery worker's wife from the 1950s, and a logger from the 1980s. We showed a short video on union history, *Born on the 28th of November: A CEP History*, sketching the origins and struggles of workers in the sectors that had come together to create the CEP, and several of us took our turns briefly at the mikes, providing perspectives and outlining plans for the new education program. Later we walked out of the hall, carrying picket signs displaying one letter each, all of them together spelling out the word "education." The crowd cheered and clapped along with the music for our exit. This rather different report of the ten-month-old CEP National Education Committee was a hit.

Taking the time to savour our accomplishments and recognize our collective talent is something we do all too rarely in union life. Yet I think we managed to do that in the "education skit," largely because Bob was willing to risk embarrassment and ridicule by being theatrical. The skit as a whole displayed the diversity of regions, cultures, languages, and races in the union, making the point that this diversity was a resource rather than a threat. The event made members feel proud of themselves and their organization.

That morning a new group had joined our convention. NABET, the National Association of Broadcast Employees and Technicians, representing camera people in television stations, had just merged with the CEP. For these new members, broadcast media people, their first morning in a CEP assembly had been capped by our theatrical production – which three of their members had helped to stage – and they must have felt right at home. By that time, so did I.

Over the previous year I had participated in shaping the educational work of a new union, joining with others to make it greater than the sum of its parts. Now its parts were even more diverse and, especially given the symbolism of NABET joining in with the rest of us, I had the sense that the next wave of union education in the CEP would not just have communications technology in it, but also heart – and even more creative sparks.

MAYWORKS, AND MORE

The Mayworks Festival has been perhaps the best example of those sparks – the blend of union and arts creativity that we had started much earlier on. Conceived by writer and arts producer Catherine Macleod after a 1985 visit to the Mayfest held in Glasgow, Scotland, the Mayworks Festival has been running since 1986. From its Toronto origins it has extended to other centres, including Ottawa and Vancouver. Although it remains a relatively small venture, a "lab" for testing new ideas and building new networks, Mayworks has presented an extraordinary array of media and content: murals, street banners, classical music performances, dances, films, storytelling, pop music concerts, and so on. It has become a solid showcase for arts-positive unionists and labour-positive professional artists. Mayworks builds an arts profile in unions and a validation of working-class identity in the arts community. It uses labour arts as a tool for public education, helping to break down the barriers between artists, workers, and the public and helping to break down the stereotypes of "artist" and "worker." It is a step along the path to democratizing culture.

Mayworks, though, is just one example of joint work between unions and artists. This work has also been seen in projects that reach out to the larger community, such as the Artists in the Workplace Program, the OFL trade union banner competition, and the newly established Ontario Workers Arts and Heritage Centre in Hamilton. It has been seen in Rosemary Donegan's poster series "Reflections of Our Labour" – a set of six fine art images printed by the Canadian Labour Congress and now hanging in union offices throughout the country. The collaboration was also apparent in Steven Bush and Allen Booth's *Life on the Line*, a one-actor play about the experience of unemployment that toured extensively and successfully through the union movement in the early 1980s.

A groundbreaking 1993 policy paper on arts and culture passed by the Ontario Federation of Labour reinforces the sense of this potential. The

OFL affirms the push to include "arts and cultural programs" in a wide range of labour activities and in labour education, and to encourage "the arts activities and creativity of working people" and whenever possible build on the relationship between professional artists and unionists. Perhaps most importantly for the artists, when artwork is commissioned, the OFL proposed that it and its affiliates "will pay the artists according to the scale set by their unions or associations." As well:

> The OFL also encourages its affiliates to develop a bargaining strategy to include the arts and culture in the workplace. Most workplaces lack the basic elements of artistic and cultural life. We could humanize the working environment by negotiating for exhibition and performance spaces in workplaces, time for cultural presentations and workshops as well as funding for cultural programmes.

The labour-arts connection is not necessarily easy. Unions do not at all times and in all places respect and encourage expression by their members. The vagaries of union confidence and democracy determine the ups and downs of the links to arts expression. Artists have their own, very separate, problems of survival and growth. And like all such ventures a program like Mayworks has limited funds and depends on the energy and enthusiasm of a few committed people to carry it through, year after year. The largest challenge, perhaps, is maintaining a clear focus and a growing momentum – to constantly and creatively build on, adapt, and possibly change the labour/arts vision to keep up with the times.

NINE

FUTURE TENSE:
DISCIPLINARY DILEMMAS
AND MOVEMENT BUILDING

■ ■ ■ ■

It's hard to look back on the limits of my understanding a year, five
years ago – how did I look without seeing, hear without listening? It
can be difficult to be generous to earlier selves ... yet how, except
through ourselves, do we discover what moves other people to
change?

> – Adrienne Rich, "Notes Towards a Politics of Location"

"Look, D'Arcy, be reasonable. We have a dress code for presenting arbitrations. It doesn't have to mean a suit, but it does mean a tie. It's a matter of
looking professional".

I had my own line on this matter. "Ties are for parties, for celebrations.
The people I represent don't wear ties to work, and neither will I."

Richard Long, Ontario vice-president of the CWC, was getting exasper-
ated. "The sixties ended nearly twenty years ago. What's the big deal?"

That hit close to home, but I only wavered for a moment. "Since I left
home, the only person who's told me what to wear is my mother. If this
really matters, you'll have to phone her."

Richard backed off, and I hung onto my little symbol of rebellion,
dressing neatly but never formally when I met with employers. Under
pressure and some consistent ribbing by co-workers, I hung onto the idea
that while managers got paid more, nobody could tell me what to wear to
work ... until an afternoon in late 1991 when Richard and I, with two
other CWC leaders, walked into a building in downtown Montreal. We

124

were about to talk with senior Bell Canada managers in a private meeting room at a session called the Common Interest Forum.

The doorman stopped us. "Excuse me, sir, but I'm afraid club rules require you to wear a tie."

We all looked at each other. Richard, Fred Pomeroy, and Rene Roy were all wearing ties, so they were okay. I was supposed to be presenting the union's views on training at the meeting, and I knew this was no time to mess around. I asked the doorman if the club could lend me a tie. But there was another problem.

"Actually, sir," the doorman said, "club rules don't allow leather jackets either." My leather jacket was stylish, and not inexpensive, but apparently it wouldn't do. "Sorry, that's the rule."

In a couple of moments I had tied on a dull brown tie and squeezed into an ill-fitting jacket. Richard Long put

Richard Long, marching in the rain at the 1993 Toronto Labour Day parade.

his hand on my shoulder and grinned: "You look terrific." With all three of my companions teasing me good-naturedly, we headed into the meeting. More was at stake than wardrobe.[1]

Some of the disciplines of union life are as simple as this. They can be put on and taken off. Others cut more deeply to the way we conduct ourselves day to day. Over the years, the challenges presented to me have changed, as has my view of the appropriate ways to respond. To see these changes, it might be helpful to revisit some of the dynamics of the union culture I raised earlier – in particular the dynamics of *diverse/ cohesive, informal/ accountable,* and *collective/ contentious* – and consider the difference between a steward course set up for the Steelworkers in the late 1970s and one for the CEP in the 1990s.

The members for whom I was writing courses in the late 1970s were comparatively homogeneous. Most of them worked in heavy industry or mining and had long loyalties to their union. In the mid-1990s the CEP stewards are employed in telephone offices, paper mills, and oil refineries

– quite different places. Until the merger in late 1992, they had no structural need to make decisions together. In each workplace, they experience tech change, training, and workplace reorganization differently. To stimulate or support learning across this kind of diversity is not the same as negotiating a benefit, like severance pay or pensions. Learning is not easily quantified and regulated. It is a voluntary act, intimately linked to personal motivation.

As the complex issue of streaming in schools has shown, simply ensuring equal access to an education program gives little assurance of equity in outcomes. Indeed, the members with greatest needs are usually those with least internal political clout. Genuine equity requires innovative financing, sensitive counselling, a democratized course-design process, and a broad range of choices for individuals and groups within the union. None of these are easy to institutionalize, nor is equity in outcomes easy to ensure. We can succeed, for example, in ensuring that all employees in a workplace receive a week of training on computer literacy. But if, for instance, a worker has no basic math, no typing experience, a back ailment, and an unemployed spouse, the experience of that week will almost certainly be utterly different from that of a co-worker who has the educational background and typing experience, no back problems, and an employed spouse. Because educational and cultural capital, like financial capital, tends to concentrate, the challenge of equity in these areas is profound.

A main goal of the CEP's education program is to build the merger at the grassroots level – to develop cohesion out of diversity. The disciplines necessary to the design, promotion, and facilitation of such a program are very different from those of fifteen years ago.

The dynamic of informal/ accountable is also very different for me today. Most collective bargaining in English Canada is directly accountable to a specific membership, while the benefits of a broad education program are widely diffused. In a training initiative like the Sectoral Skills Council, for example, less than half the workers covered are in a union, let alone in the CEP. Similarly, our sporadic efforts to develop labour-positive curriculum in the schools should help the next generation of workers to be more union-sympathetic, but the work has little immediate impact on those whose dues pay my salary. The increasing breadth of learning needs felt by workers runs directly counter to a union structure anchored in locals. For me a key discipline is to balance these broader activities with the immediate needs of new stewards for training. With limited resources and time, the tendency is for "back to basics" thinking, rather than the more innovative and future-oriented educational programming that effective unionism requires. In an increasingly volatile labour market, many workers move among workplaces. Union mergers, sectoral agreements, and legislative entitlements might help to restore accountability, but only if they are structured with that in mind. In this sense, the dynamic of informal/ accountable is playing out differently than in the past.

The subordinate/ adversarial stance of unions is also being challenged. There are continuous calls for labour to enter into "partnership" with management and government. Yet the union educator's role is precisely to sustain the adversarial stance until the subordination is removed. Here the "Three I's" – involvement, identity, and independence – should come into play.

Under current arrangements, employers rarely share what they know about future plans for the workplace, including the needs for tech change and training for it. At this point, we lack the skills and resources to address the diverse learning needs and learning styles of our members. As a result we lack the two key tools for effective educational planning: detailed knowledge of the work environment and of the potential course participants. If we don't want educational planning to be a unilateral management right, we need to develop these two tools within our own organizations. In this respect, the "three I's" stance sets the terms of our participation in partnerships, so that they will work to the benefit of the membership.

Each of these aspects of the union culture, then, acts as a discipline on union educators, and as a challenge to our collective creativity. Here are the seeds of an educational vision adequate to the changing needs of the labour movement. As we exhort companies and governments to change, we must be willing to change ourselves. The goal of social unionism is to make the labour movement into the organizational core of the social resistance in Canada. Developing these proposals requires dialogue among people who are willing to dream but are aware of the obstacles to realizing their dreams – people willing to be one of those "conscious romantics" I spoke about earlier.

Education is only a secondary part of the union vision, but it is a legitimate part requiring attention and development. Because education staff are assigned to work day by day with members, and yet need not court their votes, we have a particular contribution to make to internal discussion and debate. The elected leadership is central to the movement, but isn't the sole repository of wisdom about its dynamics. Unless staff too take responsibility for our role, we will limit the effectiveness of our social movement.

A TRIP THROUGH THE UNION STRUCTURE

A staircase, a web, and a channel: in my work in the labour movement I use these three images to help explain how the union structure operates most effectively.

The image of the *staircase* relates to the core structures of worker representation: the leadership positions to which members are elected. The *web* refers to the informal links of trust and respect that are built among people in the course of union work. The *channel* symbolizes the issues that activists become committed to in union campaigns.

These three images reflect the amazing variety of paths followed by individuals once they become active in the labour movement. All three paths co-exist in the union culture and in my own work. Their interplay forms the biochemistry of a living, evolving, renewing social movement.

Sometimes a union's stairway is steep and narrow; only skilled competitors can climb up its steps. Sometimes the steps are less steep and there is a wider space on which members can linger and relax. In any case, there is a clear hierarchy, defined responsibilities, and a visible electoral accountability. An interested member can go up the many steps: from steward to chief steward to local union officer to local president, staff representative, or national officer. Someone who wants to get into one of these positions either waits for incumbents to step aside or enters an election. On occasion a person can skip a step or two in the climb – or can take a tumble back down.

The union campaigners can be found on the staircase. They talk about personal rivalries, about whose political capital and visibility are rising or falling. The more intellectually inclined among them express the divisions in terms of policy positions. A key value on the staircase is loyalty – to individual elected leaders and to specific union organizations. The working assumption is that friends will be rewarded and enemies punished, and much effort goes into figuring out who is which.

Personally, when I think about the staircase, I know that I have a good number of allies on it, and almost no close friends. Yet I know that other union staff and I turn to the staircase people, as individuals and as a group, for our political leadership. When they are skilful and principled, we draw inspiration and guidance. When they are wilful and malicious, we seek shelter and avoidance. In either case, they cannot be ignored. The electoral staircase remains the central political focus of the movement.

The web functions differently. It is a collective product, built of co-operation rather than rivalry. In some unions it is delicate, easily damaged by hurts and betrayals. In other times and places, it is more resilient, more supported by a history of shared values and experiences. In any case, this is a widely cast network of mutual help and affection, which might be hard to grasp but has a surprising strength.

The conscious romantics can be found on the web. They talk about personal dreams, about where the energy and imagination of the movement is currently located. The more intellectually inclined among them avoid the formal policy debates and work through committees and task groups to develop new areas of consensus. A key value on the web is openness – especially to new terrains that can generate nourishing information and images. The working assumption is that friendships will survive policy and positional differences. As much effort goes into locating fun as into locating power.

Those who are bored or repelled by the staircase, yet committed to union values, find their place in the web, leading committees in local unions or project teams in national unions. The staircase people regard them with a mix of envy and condescension.

I am most at home in the web. Yet I know that my position there relies upon access to the staircase, both giving to and taking from it. Healthy unionism sustains both places, weaving discipline and innovation into a powerful cultural force. When the web is effective, it supplies vision and outreach to the union structure, scouting the sources of energy and opportunity for the next wave of worker organizing. Far-sighted union leaders turn to us for a sense of what should happen next. When we are skilful and principled, we uncover the positive potentials for labour in establishment initiatives like mass media, job training, and even adult education. When we are bitter or self-indulgent, we waste the extraordinary opportunity to incubate the ideas and images needed for workers to have more dignity and voice and beauty in their lives.

The image of the channel relates to another perspective on the future of unions. With a TV channel or a river channel in mind, I use this to refer to the grassroots experts on women's rights, occupational health, anti-racism, personal counselling, environmental issues, and so on. In some unions the channels are few and narrow, because incumbent leaders somehow manage to contain the curiosity and breadth of interests among the membership. In other times and places the range of channels is richly diverse and supportive. Channels allow strong working-class individuals to be supported in a strong union culture.

The idea of the channel relates to interests more than ambitions. Thus, for example, a new activist might have a flair for or an interest in science and be drawn into a safety and health committee in the workplace. After taking courses and attending conferences on this topic, he or she might begin to write in union publications, to instruct introductory courses for other unionists, to sit as a union representative on government consultative structures, and to work full-time in a clinic based either in the labour movement or the community.

As part of this networking, unionists today can focus their activity on coalition work. If, for example, a female union member has a personal commitment and background on women's rights, she could become active in a women's committee inside her affiliate and move from there into a women's committee in a central labour body. From there she might see a range of possible coalition activity: child care, pay equity, employment equity, reproductive choice, and arts, for instance. Depending on available time, energy, talent, and organizational backing, a union activist might come to play a significant role in these coalition activities. Later on she might gain employment in a women's organization, outside the labour movement and far from the original workplace that had led her to join the union in the first place.

The most determined and effective union innovators are often found in the channels. They talk about their interests with an intensity of focus that disturbs the staircase people, who see them as "one-issue" unionists. The more intellectually inclined among them formulate resolutions and plans around their interests and push for the adoption of those proposals. Sometimes, after they achieve their goals in an area of interest, they return to their union committees and pursue alliances with others outside the unions. The key value on this spectrum of channels is choice. It is possible to go down a path that other unionists may not yet consider a priority. The working assumption is that unions are elastic, that the range of legitimate union concern can and should broaden.

If personal recovery and the environment are important issues, and unions are engaged in important issues, so the argument goes, then unions should be engaged in personal recovery and environment. This logic is so clear to people in the channels that they are genuinely perplexed when union leaders speak of the need for focus and discipline and unity in ways that exclude those issues. The people who have chosen certain channels, then, are less interested in the power of position than are those on the staircase. They are less immersed in the union culture and its values than are the people on the web, and less interested in working towards consensus. While the staircase people try to cut deals with them, and the web people try to broaden their interests, the assertiveness and autonomy of the channel people disrupt both the staircase and the web.

The channels rely upon the existence of the staircase and the web to continue as part of the labour movement. A strong and accountable electoral core and a lively, innovative network of engaged unionists sustain the channels that members want to follow. Without that access they could find other community or public terrains for their work, but this would result in a loss of dedication and diversity inside the unions. If unions continue to rely on traditional formulas of "strength through unity" without accommodating the increasing range of interests among the members, the structures will gradually wither. The unions will die of boredom. But to the degree that union leaders can reach out to take in the social passion of members committed to causes that have not been traditional issues, they will ensure the future vitality of the movement.

A healthy unionism welcomes all three kinds of involvement. On the staircase some members find a platform and a mission for articulating their co-workers' interests. In the web members build the consensus and cultural cohesion so necessary to maintain the overall structure. In the channels members seek out and engage with social issues affecting their lives.

While each of these images has its own potential internally, the fascination of union life lies in their interaction. In a union course I usually find a few participants who fit neatly into one or another of these categories, and the dynamic among them helps to provide the energy of the class. I also find that the most effective activists draw some comfort from all three.

THE CHALLENGE OF OPEN-FIELD BARGAINING

The experience of doing educational work on management styles, tech change, and training has changed my thinking about union education as well as my willingness to dress up. For instance, my early educational work in the back to the locals program was to strengthen a structure whose goals and identity were clear. But that was in "initiation time," in the late 1970s. One thing I have since found out is that unionism has to be redefined, over and over, according to the times.

There is a lot of learning to be done, by new union activists, union appointees, and union leaders. For support in this learning, people often turn to the educator on their staff. And that educator looks up from the steward training manuals, pushes aside a script for a video on running union meetings, and says, "Let's have a look." Another round of learning is about to begin for the educator as well.

Union activists have always looked to broader social change, but the focus of daily work has been the collective bargaining relationship, the immediate contact with the employer. During the late 1970s an activist could be entirely involved in this sphere alone. The restructuring of the economy since then has shaken both the workplace and the community, and unions have been obliged to change, to merge, to reorganize internally.

Unions are now involved in a great web of consultative and decision-making bodies. And when a central labour body speaks to its corresponding level of government, it is joined formally and informally by a network of church, community, and social movement organizations. As a result, union leaders have new responsibilities. An elected union leader has always had to represent the members in public, but now such representation includes a range of media and formal structures that unionists were excluded from in the past.

A national officer of a union receives invitations every month to join a committee on a matter of public interest. The link to the members' interests may be indirect, and the topic very distant from his or her personal interests and background. The task may place them at a table between a university president and an advocate for people with disabilities. In front of them on the table they may find sheafs of documents that don't at all resemble the negotiating and political action texts that were central to an earlier generation of union activists.

The learning needed for coalition building and social bargaining is essential to the future of the union movement. Labour's role in coalitions may not be as the visionary leadership – that can be left, perhaps, to the artists and poets, to the prophetic popular religious organizations, or academic theorists. What unions are good at is organizing, networking – getting people involved – and in general building the structures to face power.

Unlike a lot of social action groups, unions have long experience of direct and frequent face-to-face confrontation with the economic establishment. Consciousness-raising is a part of what we do, but it is not the final purpose of what we do – that is to win more power for workers. Our orientation to the problems of power is both a strength and a weakness in coalition-building. How power really works is not something that a lot of the more visionary elements of the social opposition like talking about. The ambivalence of the social opposition around power is one of its greatest weaknesses. Here, unions bring something constructive to the conversation.

132

Yet in these discussions, the tendency for labour to stand up for itself is problematic. The scrappiness, the anger, the pain that working people feel is expressed by their unions in open-field bargaining, and it offends people. But without this edge of passion, our credibility with the membership would be lost. Perhaps we just have to do it, and pay the price.

In some situations, the appropriate mode of conduct is one of "contained combat." While this sounds harsh, contained combat is an honourable pattern in our society. It is the basis, for example, of all our parliamentary institutions. All elected representatives there accept the rules. In this sense there is a partnership among the Liberals, the Tories, the NDP, the Reform Party, and the Bloc Québécois. None of these parties dissolves its identity, and the basis of struggle is win/ lose. Most wage bargaining operates on the same basis.

In open-field bargaining there is a time and place for consensus, for blending our identities, for going it together. This is most clear in coalitions, such as those seeking to improve child care or to retain medicare.

I have watched open-field bargaining in which the union representatives follow the rules precisely, picking away at details until someone else explodes and the time is ripe to have the basic issue properly heard. I have heard union representatives cryptically tip one another off to a problem in a public meeting, and then begin to build on one another's comments gradually, not frontally attacking the dominant view but cumulatively making it look absurd. These tactics, developed in facing power in the workplace, are valuable in broader arenas. By following out along the web, through the channel, and up the staircase, labour representatives can develop a route to influence the broader economic and political environment – and not just clean up the results of the dominant agenda.

Momentum, the Chinese philosopher Sun Tzu wrote two thousand years ago, is like rushing water, which can move huge rocks and change entire landscapes.[2] Timing is like the swoop of the falcon, precise in its judgement of when to make a move. To develop our strategy, then, we need to make use of the direction and speed of momentum and accurately judge the right time for action. At times unionists should choose to be combative. At other times we should choose to be collaborative, because it suits our goals. The style of operation shouldn't be a matter of personality traits or a moral imperative, but a calm, collective choice based on objectives combined with a clear sense of momentum and timing.

When mainstream consultants lecture us on the merits of co-operation and win/ win negotiations, we must bear in mind that unions have often caused conflicts, and that we have made our greatest gains through conflict and struggle. Conflict is not intrinsically violent, nor is it anarchic. Here we can build on our experience of labour-management relations. Those relations follow certain rules, and the parties involved expect those rules to be respected. If, for example, a union committee agrees to recommend a negotiated settlement to the members and then undermines it at the ratification meetings, management legitimately feels betrayed. Or if negotiators reach a tentative agreement and the decision is overturned by higher-ups, unionists don't just feel irritated – they feel the rules have been violated.

Management representatives in negotiated joint programs like the Sectoral Skills Council, at both the workplace and the sectoral level, have always preferred the language of "joint" participation and "teamwork" over a clear recognition of divergent interests. But we should be affirming our union identity and our adversarial tradition, not dissolving it in an abstract commitment to "joint" participation or "partnership." Interestingly, some of the most successful joint initiatives around new work systems follow protracted conflict. The worker ownership program at Algoma Steel in Sault Ste. Marie followed on a strike, as did a co-operative venture at Saskatchewan Chemical. For that matter, the whole structure of co-management in Sweden followed years of bitter labour-management battles.3

Managers and government leaders have been following the advice of Sun Tzu for some time now. Among unionists this approach is a lot more common than it was when I started doing worker education in the late 1970s. Yet the pattern of subordinate and adversarial behaviour remains a defining feature of the union culture. Adopting the new information, attitudes, and skills required for a strategic approach to open-field bargaining is a challenge for the labour movement. Certainly the union educator has a role to play in equipping people for this new mode of representing fellow employees.

As we look ahead, each union educator will have to assess the momentum and timing for supporting such learning, and plan strategy accordingly. Personally, I am opting for direct involvement in coalitions such as labour-arts and in social bargaining such as the Sectoral Skills Council. My hope is that these joint organizational and educational initiatives will not just extend the influence of the union but also help preserve its identity and independence.

THINKING TWICE: IT'S ALRIGHT

On the surface it was just another book launch: a couple of hundred people gathered in a bar in Toronto in late 1994 to celebrate the release of yet another new book. The book, written by David Sobel and Susan Meurer, detailed the history of workers at the Toronto plant of Inglis Limited – treating that little known history in great depth and with intense respect for the workers.[4] As both a unionist and an expectant author myself I was glad to be there, but I didn't expect to find the strong sense of community that the evening would bring.

The crowd was large and noisy, including many former Inglis employees, local union officers, and Lynn Williams, the recently retired international president of the Steelworkers. Eight years earlier Lynn had ensured that I was fired from that union. At the book launch we remembered that time in a friendly enough way, without either of us giving any ground on the matter. Lynn remarked that a future generation would have to make the decision as to which of us was right at that time. Then we laughed, realizing our joint stubbornness. Both of us were still convinced that we were right.

Lynn expressed a genuine interest in my current work, and his questioning was as sharp and insightful as ever. We spoke of forgiveness. He was the last of the people central to my firing with whom I made peace, and it was a relief.

I cast my eye around the room, crowded with people I had taught and others who had taught me fifteen years earlier, and knew that I belonged here among these unionists and committed activists, people there to celebrate the union culture they had helped to build.

Returning home late that night, I scribbled a reminder to write about my feelings. I was still feeling the effects of the cigarette smoke, a little light-headed from the beer, agitated from the encounter with Lynn Williams, but in the end I was feeling quietly comfortable with it all – with the labour movement and with myself. I thought of the wealth of experience, insight, and passion in that room, and about how much those people had contributed to the country – and how much more they could offer if given half the chance.

Curiously, that evening seemed to bring together a number of issues I had been working on in my analysis of union life and union education. It reminded me that the changes needed in unions are not just structural. Each of us who has chosen to build the labour movement has personal changes to make as well. As the next wave of leadership gathers its strength, and spreads across the staircase, the web, and the channels of union building, it seems to me that there are at least five themes we should be discussing.

The first is *identity*. Unionists are constituted by their social identity, their organizational identity, and their political identity.6 In my courses I work with people becoming active in unions, beginning to identify themselves with the union culture. This has been my own process as well. The split in my organizational identity, between educator and unionist, was a clash of affiliations in the early years. While it was settled in favour of unionism, it remains a tension in my work and in the varied people around me.

Then there is the importance of *historical awareness*. It seems to me that for labour a shift is under way, from the centrality of collective bargaining to the dynamics of workplace reorganization and social bargaining. The current challenge for union educators is to democratize these new forms of union action in ways that attract new activists and renew the movement's effectiveness.

A third theme is *process politics*.7 I have drawn some of the lessons needed to promote a learning agenda within a highly politicized popular movement. Yet within labour itself, the skills of participatory decision-making, of democratic communication, of simple good listening, are spread thin. While some of my own learning in this area has been painful, its application has been a source of strength and satisfaction. In a time when employers are re-engineering their structures, by emphasizing process rather than task, it behooves the union leadership to consider process as a focus of their attention.

Personal and organizational renewal is a fourth theme.8 Educational practice needs to help develop the imagination. In labour we need creative effort to sustain the spirit while we both resist and develop alternatives to the dominant culture. The educator in a social movement is uniquely positioned both to recognize the need for such renewal and to assist in bringing it about.

The fifth theme is the *critical spirit* – that impulse to reflect on social practice as well as to engage in it. This requires a certain personal and political distance from activists for whom such reflection is disturbing or even threatening – leaving the critic apart and united, *solitaire et solidaire*.

These five themes – awareness of identity, analysis of the historical moment, political commitment and skill, a developed imagination, and a critical spirit – emerge from my experience. These same themes will also, I hope, help form the pathway into my next decade or two of work as a political educator.

■ ■ ■ ■

During the week before submitting the final manuscript of this book I was weary and irritable. I was working full days and spending three or four hours each evening trying to clarify and improve the text. On a hot Saturday morning in July, then, I felt grumpy about having to drive to the east end of Hamilton for a membership meeting of a CEP local.

My friend Ed Vance, a militant promoter of workers' health and safety since his Steelworker days in the mines of Elliot Lake, had suggested I attend. He would be speaking to the meeting, and he thought I could get some of the members involved in the new Ontario Workers Arts and Heritage Centre. We

Ed Vance, shown here in a health and safety meeting at the Steelworkers in 1980.

had just purchased the old Custom House in Hamilton as a headquarters and needed more unionists involved in its programs. It seemed this would be a good chance to spread the word in the community as well as within my own union.

Not surprisingly, turnout on a sunny Saturday was low – ten members from a workplace of ninety – and the meeting's chair told us he had golf clubs in the trunk of his car and wanted the meeting over in an hour and a half. Ed and I kept our pitches under ten minutes each. For the rest of the meeting I settled back to listen, and gradually my fatigue lifted.

The ten unionists were discussing the situation of a long-time employee who had spent the last four years in management. The workplace had been non-union until a year earlier, and the union members were still getting used to having a collective voice on the job. In this particular case, the employee was being moved back into the bargaining unit, where by logic she should start over with the lowest seniority. But some of her co-workers felt she had been badly enough treated already and that the union should show compassion by granting her full seniority.

Artwork by the late dian marino, reflecting her world view in 1984.

The discussion continued for over half an hour, as the members checked whether this special consideration would set a precedent for future situations. It might, for instance, encourage management to promote and demote in an arbitrary way. Two women at the meeting were employed in the same work area, and they would be directly affected: if seniority were granted, during a slow period they might be laid off while this other person would be kept on. They had to consider whether they were willing to take the risk.

In the end the meeting unanimously decided that the union would seek full seniority for the worker, both in the department and across the company. Someone said, "We'd better be ready to take some flak on the floor over this, from the people who will resent her coming back in at top wage and top seniority." One of the women directly affected smiled and said, "We just made a unanimous decision, and we all know we're doing the right thing. Those narrow-minded people had better start showing up at their union meetings."

Without any more fuss the chair moved on to the next item. But I was suddenly, quietly, glad I had come that morning. Here was a group of workers making decisions in a careful and informed manner – decisions that would have an impact on their rights on the job.

The next item promised even less drama. One member was concerned about the role of favouritism in people being moved to the higher-skill and higher-wage jobs in the plant. It seemed management had a habit of training their favourite people, and then when a promotion was available they could say that one of these favoured people had higher qualifications than a more senior person. In this way they were making a mockery of seniority, and the member was frustrated: "That's the kind of crap we brought the union in to stop, and it turns out the union can't do anything about it."

The union rep, Ken Cole, spoke up, noting that any first contract had holes in it. "In the next round of bargaining we just need to add a clause saying that experience and training acquired during temporary transfers can't be considered in later job postings." A woman sitting next to me nodded vigorously and said that would fix the problem. Then Ed Vance, quiet until then, jumped in. "In the meantime," he said, "keep grieving every time they do this, so that you have a record of the problem when you get into the next round of contract negotiations." Now everyone was nodding, seeing how they could gradually strengthen their voice on the job by using this new tool, the union.

The meeting ran a few minutes longer than the hour and a half expected, but all of us left in a good mood. Ed Vance came over to me, smiling. "Wasn't that great?" We agreed that we had once again seen what a union local was really like, what it could really do – and we had been reminded of the importance of work at the grassroots level. "Sometimes we forget what all this is for," Ed said to me. "But this morning brought it all back, just like when I first got involved."

My first involvement wasn't quite like Ed's. When I started at the Steelworkers, my image of unionism was much more dramatic, more ideological than it is now. Almost two decades later, I find it inspiring to see a small group of workers shifting the balance of power in their workplace by collective action. They were open to the wider action of the union movement, both in occupational health and safety and in arts and heritage. This particular morning had been well spent. And I felt strongly that, to the degree that I had contributed to democratizing the labour movement, and through it the workplace, my years in the labour movement had also been well spent.

Despite occasional anger at others, or frustration with myself, I never cease to be amazed and excited by the learning provided to me by the grounded and passionate union culture. I know the union movement is not perfect, but it is the most rich, satisfying, and caring learning environment I have ever encountered. That is why I plan to stay, why I plan to go on working at union education, helping to prepare the next generation of leaders and to get ready for the next wave of changes, both personal and political.

READERS' COMMENTS

■ ■ ■ ■

As this manuscript evolved, I asked a number of friends and colleagues for comments. Their input has often found its way into the final text. Following are excerpts from a few longer statements I received from a variety of locations in the labour movement.

1. From Vancouver

With old age you are showing some diplomacy in this text. There is something about maturity that is scary, but it should still cause some people to look into their mirror and reflect. I do see in it the Golden Triangle Syndrome, since most of the book is centred in the middle of the universe. . . . I wonder how different the politics of union education are in Quebec and the East, and for that matter from Manitoba west.

This book documents most of the speed bumps and pot holes on the road to self-actualization. I found it interesting because of our past working relationships – this being a time in both our lives when we knew where we wanted to go but chose somewhat different road maps to get there. Neither has been as slippery as the highway from Faro to Whitehorse that we drove together. But this text gave me a glimpse of another D'Arcy Martin who never totally showed his hopes and fears before.

    – Don Posnick, Education Representative, District 3, United Steelworkers of America

2. From Timmins

You've captured the instructor in me with this book – the down to earth part – the good, the bad, and the ugly. It brings home to me some of my difficulties as an educator, and the good times too.

As a woman in a Leader/ Educator position having to put up with the old male mentality, I identified with your personal transition – your difficulties as a family member being torn apart by our work as trade unionists. It was refreshing to see you work it through with women's issues still a large part of your agenda.

Family ties and the children . . . "is this the union?" How do we define the union to our children? How true that our kids don't understand what we do. The union, and our passion for it, is not concrete to them. I was once told that I was married to my union. That may just be so. Educators are like that, aren't we?

— *Claire Duthie, Education Co-ordinator, Local 6,* CEP

3. From Ottawa

I paid especially close attention to your description of coming to terms in the early eighties, when the basic steel industry was decimated. There are uncomfortable parallels with the turmoil we now face at CUPE.

For the first time in the union's existence, CUPE members working in municipalities, school boards, hospitals, and community services are facing deep spending cuts and widespread layoffs. Working within a culture and structure shaped by rapid membership growth, we are now struggling to respond to a dramatically changed set of demands.

What I like about your description is how you highlight the personal reality of working within an organization under fire. While our conversations are about new strategies and tactics, I often doubt my own abilities and vision. As you've said, it is often tempting to just get through the day – go through the motions, retreat to a safe corner – and avoid the self-criticism and reflection that are necessary to thinking through new directions.

I think this is true at the policy level as well as at the personal level. For instance, there was very little discussion (that I know of) after we were defeated in the campaigns against the GST and NAFTA. We need places for honest self-criticism and discussion in order to take stock of what we have learned from defeats such as these.

— *Matt Sanger, Research Department, Canadian Union of Public Employees*

4. From Toronto

On our long runs through the hills of Periopolis, near the Steelworkers' Education Centre at Linden Hall in 1984–85, I always marvelled at how foolhardy D'Arcy was in thinking he could openly support Dave Patterson for District 6 Director and not pay the price. How long did he think that he could survive at the National Office should Patterson lose? At least I could remain as president of local 2900, until Whirlpool Corporation took care of that by closing the Toronto Inglis plant.

It is interesting to note that most Steelworkers from all political factions, in hindsight, now view the removal of D'Arcy from the Education Department as one of the dark days in Steelworker history. But in reading through his book, it is nice to know he has learned a few lessons, lest he suffer the same fate elsewhere. This is not to say that he should compromise his principles, only that as a "pork chopper," the label for staff reps that he often applies to himself, he needs to be a bit more discreet.

In the concluding chapter, he mentions the Inglis reunion and book launch held in October, 1994. There, D'Arcy made peace with Lynn Williams, former International President of the Steelworkers and a dues-paying member of Local 2900, who, D'Arcy claims, "had ensured that [he] was fired from that union." He could have further added that in the same room were all the previously conflicting factions of the union, the Patterson supporters, and the Establishment. And everyone "belonged."

You can throw away your 1984 score book; the game has changed and the union has moved on. Part of that is due to the political adroitness of Leo Gerard and his successors in bringing together all the previously conflicting factions within the union, but much of it is simply that the issues have changed. NAFTA, support for Bob Rae and the NDP, and the current attack on social programs from all levels of government have altered the political forces not only within the Steelworkers, but within the entire Canadian trade union movement.

The "strong sense of community" that we all felt at the Inglis event is why we became trade union activists, in spite of the shifting internal politics. D'Arcy has made and continues to make significant contributions to this community, and this book is one of them.

> – *Mike Hersh, Former President, Local 2900, USWA, and currently Senior Coordinator, Canadian Steel Trade and Employment Congress*

5. From Ottawa

Many people are teachers, but the union educator is a special category of teacher. Many people are union reps, but developing and leading union courses is much different from servicing, negotiating, handling grievances, solving health and safety problems – the usual kinds of union rep activity.

Union educators have a unique blend of the practical and the philosophical in their work. The unionist on a steward course needs to know the practical side of grievance handling – what the contract says, how to fill in the grievance form – but must also be equipped to deal with moral questions – should we represent the guilty, who should we support when two members' interests are in conflict, and so on.

The union educator does not teach this. Rather, she or he leads the participants to find the correct answers themselves, helping them navigate a stream of dangerous waters – interpersonal difficulties, political stances, internal union conflicts – exhilarating as you pass through, but potentially very threatening if you misread the waters and paddle the wrong way.

All this happens within a framework provided by the union's constitution and policies, which too may be called into question by the participants, members of the union themselves.

> – *Bob Hatfield, Education Director, CEP*

6. From Hamilton

When you wrote about relating to other groups and activists, I was reminded of a saying that "with knowledge comes responsibility." Of course, a further line could be added: "with acknowledged responsibility comes loss."

Your remarks about the oral culture of unionists suggest that it is rare to record events and meetings on paper. This reminded me of just how rarely I take paper and pen into a meeting. I had always assumed I was just a bit lazy. In truth I had never thought about it before now.

Your turmoil about the union staff layoffs reminded me of a time in 1966 when I was number 506 on a cut list which axed 500 jobs at the CNR Machine Shop in Moncton, New Brunswick. The cut meant I had to move, but I still had a job. I did develop a real dislike for federal politicians as a result. We held a support rally at the local hockey arena, and David Lewis, then leader of the NDP, came down and spoke eloquently against the cuts. He went back to Ottawa and we never heard from him again. I took years to get over that sense of being used and forgotten.

– Wayne Marston, President, Local 42, CEP

7. From Toronto

My formal link with the Toronto labour movement started in 1977, when I became an organizer with the International Ladies Garment Workers Union. That was a year before D'Arcy's narrative begins. Since then, I have worked as a labour educator, as co-ordinator of an English in the Workplace program, and as a card-carrying trade unionist.

Throughout all these years, I saw my work as building coalitions between community and labour, as part and parcel of a broader framework of anti-racism. For when immigrant women workers, workers of colour, risk their livelihood to sign union cards, it is more than just a fight for fair wages. They are taking a united stand for dignity and an end to racism in their workplaces. The work of many of us as workers of colour in the labour movement has been one of trying to create space and challenging the labour movement to look beyond the interests of class.

There is an almost blind belief among trade unionists that as long as we can dismantle the capitalist economy, all social ills will disappear. Yet in a labour movement that is predominantly white and male, solidarity exists for some, but not for many. As one who is a sister, but still an outsider, I can see that the periods of my work break down somewhat differently from D'Arcy's, into four periods:

- 1975–80 – poor immigrant women/ language over race
- 1980–85 – racism hurts everyone
- 1985–90 – a fragile coalition
- 1990–today – backlash against employment equity.

We need tools to seek solace, to gather strength, and to move forward. In my experience, writing has this potential. As we engage in it, we must remember that unity does not mean unanimity. Recognizing the strength of our differences and the common localities of our struggle will move us forward. Genuine democratic education within the labour movement can contribute greatly to creating safe spaces, to articulating differences, and to defining common ground.

– Winnie Wun Wun Ng, feminist and anti-racist activist

8. From Cobourg, Ontario

When I finished reading this manuscript, I thought how tough it is right now, in a climate of recession and cutbacks, to sustain what you and I have worked to build. Governments are cutting back education, even including the federal grant to the CLC. Even within the labour movement, the pressure of shrinking budgets tends to put education as a secondary priority. Where are the voices to cry out for education, and how do we get to them, to help them make the noise?

A member with a grievance just wants a simple statement on paper, and a clear yes or no from management. But the steward has to write carefully, seeking full redress and beginning to engage in the language of persuasion and joint problem-solving. Education is required for this to work. Unionism today is so complex that activists need more than a basic grievance-handling course. Twenty years ago, that's all most of us got and it was enough. Today, without strong reading skills and communications skills, we just can't be effective. Many people still think they can take a union position without any training or preparation, which puts a lot of pressure on everyone.

In my area, we have produced paintings, musical events, plays, a video, and a banner. Yet still, most of our members see no relevance in this work. They have lived so long without art, without any portrait or documentation of their lives, that they see no value in it. For rank and file members, neither the union nor the arts is as central to their lives as it is for you.

It is personally risky to speak out. There can be hurt here, both for the giver and the receiver. I hope we can keep from becoming defensive, because it would set us all back.

– Linda Mackenzie-Nicholas, president, Local 534 of CEP
and Northumberland and District Labour Council

9. From Burnaby, B.C.

I identified with your feeling of being the outsider, the sense of inadequacy and awe and also awareness. I wonder if this is one of the conditions of being an educator – someone who sees from two places at once and wants to foster dialogue?

I have been an outsider since I was ten, the only Westerner in my Montreal elementary school, an anglophone in Quebec. And in construction you can't be the only woman without educating the men, answering their questions over and over (*why are you here?*). The first time I went to a B.C. Federation of Labour convention, I stopped dead inside the doors when I smelled not sweat or Old Spice, but genuine French perfume. There were other women here. I felt as if I'd come home.

But it wasn't easy. When I taught women, I was a construction worker, and they were office or service or health-care workers. I thought screaming matches with the foreman and pounding on cars on picket lines were normal. I was amazed at how polite women were, how restrained. I was still an outsider.

And now, as director of a university labour program, I am "labour" to the academic community and "university" to labour. I don't regret this. In many ways an outsider can see some things better than an insider. The outsider is also given certain permissions that insiders are not.

I really like that you distinguish the labour movement with the name "culture." I like the implication that we are an identifiable people with a history and a language of our own. I also like the artistic connotations of culture. We *have* a culture, as well as being one.

The quality of being at once diverse and cohesive is one of the keys to the success of the women's movement, where it is a source of strength. It shows in the Summer Institute for Union Women, an annual event since 1992 involving about 200 women. We affirm the rights of the previously oppressed, of lesbians, women of colour, and First Nations women, and women in general – encourage the powerless to take power. Then we struggle to handle it, to focus it constructively when they try it out on us, the organizers, first. This is a balance that we actively and imperfectly seek to maintain each year. It makes for a hell of an intense, emotional, and exhilarating learning experience for all of us.

Also on the subject of "oppression," one of the ways it is used within the labour movement is that as women and others challenge traditional ways of doing things, some people are threatened and identify us as causing disunity. Most women have been told more than once when we stood up for something we believed in (including our own right to speak) that we were "causing disunity." Within labour that is a chilling thing to be accused of. "Causing disunity" runs in direct conflict with our spoken (and necessary) commitment to solidarity. It is a useful club for neutralizing opposition.

I agree that it was extremely positive for workers to feature labour-focused theatre and to socialize at the Harrison Winter School in British Columbia. But for many of those same years and through the same events, many women were uncomfortable. The percentage of women at the school was, I believe, not high. (The CLC Pacific Region has done a lot of work in the recent past to change that.) The parties that went on late into the night were, in a lot of cases, the hustling of women. The CLC worked with the Women's Committee of the B.C. Federation of Labour in the late eighties to make Harrison more welcoming for women. This is where reading the statement of "zero tolerance of harassment" began.

In the story of Fred Pomeroy's challenge to the Premier's Council on Technology, there is an exhilaration in your tone that I'm sure was the feeling at the time, but speaking from the distance of a few years, I think the mood has changed, at least in British Columbia. My sense of most unions on the issue of bipartite process is one of confusion and doubt and insecurity. For those who have embraced it or who are seen by other unions to have embraced it, it is somewhat defensive. I don't see increasing union "legitimacy" but a continued caution.

Likewise, your glowing description on the formation of social coalitions may be more an Eastern than a Western phenomenon. Talk of coalitions here is greeted by a large number of labour leaders with the waving of garlic and crosses. Our experience of Solidarity in 1983 is passionately remembered by all, as a highpoint of real and potential social coalition building for some, as a low point of irresponsibility and betrayal by others. Everyone was hurt by it.

But I have enormous hope for the labour movement after watching almost a thousand women go through the Summer Institute. I think women are very good at alliances because we don't have a lot of ego involved in getting things done. We have a lot of passion, a lot of anger, and a lot of communication skills. I have been touched, over and over, by women's courage in confronting difference (or difficulty) and talking through it until there is consensus.

Certainly women's voices are challenged with all the recent (and upcoming) public sector layoffs and the pressures on women to take over social and family responsibilities. But I would not say our voices have faded: the opposite. I see women working hard at the fightback – and organizing. The growth of the labour movement (at least in British Columbia) right now is because women, largely in the service sector, are signing union cards.

– Kate Braid, Co-ordinator, Labour Program, Simon Fraser University

NOTES

■　■　■　■

1. "WE SHALL TAKE OUR FREEDOM AND DANCE"

1. Adrienne Rich, *An Atlas of the Difficult World: Poems 1988–91* (New York: Norton, 1991), p.11.

2. For a breakdown of union periods, see Craig Heron, *The Canadian Labour Movement: A Short History* (Toronto: James Lorimer and Company, 1989).

3. For a forceful and eloquent set of public sector union responses to this pressure, see Jeff Rose, *Worth Fighting For: Selected Speeches and Articles, 1983–91* (Ottawa: Canadian Union of Public Employees, 1991).

4. The collapse of U.S. labour, and of the U.S. left, during this decade was part of a broader economic and social restructuring. See, for example, Lawrence Mishel and David M. Frankel, "Hard Times for Working America: Facts You Ought to Know," in *Dissent*, Vol.38, No.2 (Spring 1991). In Canada, the tone of discussion has been different. See, for example, John O'Grady, "Labour Market Policy and Industrial Strategy after the Free Trade Agreement: The Policy Debate in Ontario," paper presented to the Industrial Relations Research Association, Buffalo, New York, May 3, 1990.

5. Judy Darcy, "Foreword," in Linda Briskin and Patricia McDermott, *Women Challenging Unions: Feminism, Democracy and Militancy* (Toronto: University of Toronto Press, 1993), p.ix.

6. For useful discussion on the adult education dimension, see the special issue on "Critical Social Theory and Adult Education," *Canadian Journal for the Study of Adult Education*, Vol.v (Winter 1991). A perspective wider than the educational field is provided in Himani Bannerji, ed., *Returning the Gaze: Essays on Racism, Feminism and Politics* (Toronto: Sister Vision Press, 1993.) On the privileges and handicaps of "traditional intellectuals" in relation to the working-

class movement, and their relations with "organic intellectuals," see the
discussion of Gramsci in Jean-Marc Piotte, *La Pensee Politique de Gramsci*
(Montreal: Parti Pris, 1970), pp.45–70.

7. This is the closing part of Mario Benedetti's poem "Por Que Cantamos,"
written in Argentina at the peak of the "dirty war" against the left. It was published as part of a collection called *Cotidianas* (Mexico: Siglo Veintiuno, 1979).
This poem has since been set to music by many folk and protest singers. The
English translation is my own.

2. INITIATION TIME

1. These meetings were best documented in Ontario, where they were
assembled into a report, "Worker Education: Real Power," October 1979.

2. The sketch here only includes those unions within the "house of labour," the
Canadian Labour Congress. Since my own direct experience is limited to the
mainstream labour movement, my overview will concentrate on the educational dynamics within it. There are many independent unions, such as those
for nurses and teachers, and there are company associations such as the Canadian Telephone Employees Association, which represents clerical workers at
Bell Canada.

   The withdrawal of the construction trades from the CLC in the early 1980s
led to formation of the Canadian Federation of Labour. Further, nationalist
politics in Quebec and in English Canada kept the Confédération des Syndi-
cats Nationaux (CSN) in Quebec, and the Confederation of Canadian Unions
(CCU), mostly in British Columbia, outside the house of labour.

3. See, for example, Rick Arnold and Bev Burke, *A Popular Education Handbook:
An Educational Experience Taken from Central America and Adapted to the Canadian
Context* (Toronto/ Ottawa: Adult Education Department, OISE/CUSO Development Education, 1983); and Deborah Barndt, *To Change This House: Popular
Education under the Sandinistas* (Toronto: Between the Lines, 1991). In this
regard, Rita Kwok Hoi Yee and Arokia Dass are particularly important sources
of inspiration for me.

4. On the role of "connected critic," and for the quote from Camus, see Michael
Walzer, "Commitment and Social Criticism: Camus' Algerian War," *Dissent*,
No.137 (Fall 1984), pp.426–28.

5. From Ogden Nash, "Kind of an Ode to Duty," *The Face is Familiar* (Garden City,
N.Y.: Garden City Publishing Co., 1941), p.175.

3. UNION CULTURE: A BIRD'S EYE VIEW

1. On diversity within cultures, see Clifford Geertz, *The Interpretation of Cultures*
(New York: Basic Books, 1973). On women's experience in Canadian unions,

see Julie White, *Sisters and Solidarity: Women and Unions in Canada* (Toronto: Thompson Educational Publishing, 1993).

2. On the organizational structures of unions, see Jonas Pontusson, "Introduction: Organizational and Political-Economic Perspectives on Union Politics," in *Bargaining for Change: Union Politics in North America and Europe*, ed. Miriam Golden and Jonas Pontusson (Ithaca: Cornell University Press, 1992), especially pp.10–22. On political currents, see chapter 7 in Bryan D. Palmer, *Working Class Experience: Re-thinking the History of Canadian Labour, 1800–1991* (Toronto: McClelland and Stewart, 1992). On the textures of the work process, which run across such tensions, see Philip Levine, "They Feed the Lion," in his *Selected Poems* (New York: Atheneum, 1984), p.81.

3. Palmer, *Working Class Experience*, p.21.

4. For a powerful critique of North American individualism, see Christopher Lasch, *The Minimal Self: Psychic Survival in Troubled Times* (New York: Norton, 1984). For a discussion of how markets have eroded community, see Herman E. Daly and John B. Cobb, *For the Common Good: Redirecting the Economy Toward Community, the Environment and a Sustainable Future* (Boston: Beacon Press, 1989).

5. Briskin and McDermott, *Women Challenging Unions*, p.12.

6. These biases are systemic, and listing them here is not an accusation against any individuals in that local or the Steelworkers. Indeed, the Steelworkers across North America have been among the leaders in the labour movement in addressing racism. The issues here for white people are sketched in Peggy McIntosh, "White Privilege: Unpacking the Invisible Knapsack," *Peace and Freedom*, July/August (1989); and in Barb Thomas, "The Politics of Being White: A Letter to My Daughters," in *Talking about Difference: Encounters in Culture, Language, and Identity*, ed. Carl James and Adrienne Shadd (Toronto: Between the Lines, 1994).

7. For instance, in a series of courses offered by the Canadian Labour Congress the proportion of women receiving scholarships to attend was equivalent to the representation of women in the affiliates. In other words, the unions looked good relative to the society, while the courses looked good relative to other aspects of union life. See White, *Sisters and Solidarity*, pp.115, 149.

8. See Edelson, "The Boys Just Don't Get It," *Our Times*, vol. 13, no. 5, October-November 1994.

9. The effectiveness of such weapons can be attested to by a number of fallen union leaders. Among them, one of the most brilliant was Cec Taylor, president of Steelworkers Local 1005 in Hamilton during the 1980s. For a dramatic chronicle of his rise and fall, see Morton Ritts, "Cec and Desist," *Hamilton Magazine*, 1987.

10. While "Jim" existed, his name has been changed in this text. In the years since, overall employment at Alcan Kingston has dropped significantly. Only

high-seniority employees now remain at the plant.

11. This was obviously the case in the 1981 Steelworker elections, which brought Dave Patterson to power. Among other "surprises" during the 1980s were the election of James Clancy as president of the Ontario Public Service Employees Union and Jeff Rose as president of the Canadian Union of Public Employees.

12. The following, from Article 8, "Management Rights," in *Collective Agreement between Communications and Electrical Workers of Canada and Bell Canada, Operator Services and Dining Service Employees,* effective January 5, 1994, is typical:

> The Company has the exclusive right and power to manage its operations in all respects and in accordance with its commitments and responsibilities to the public, to conduct its business efficiently and to direct the working forces and, without limiting the generality of the foregoing, it has the exclusive right and power to hire, promote, transfer, demote or lay off employees, and to suspend, dismiss or otherwise discipline employees. The Company agrees that any exercise of these rights and powers shall not contravene the provisions of this Agreement.

For a wider, political economy perspective, see Craig Heron and Greg Kealey, "Labour Conflict and Working-Class Organization," in Daniel Drache and Wallace Clement,(eds.) *The New Practical Guide to Canadian Political Economy,*(Toronto: James Lorimer & Co., 1985.)

13. David Sobel and Susan Meurer, *Working at Inglis: The Life and Death of a Canadian Factory* (Toronto: Lorimer, 1994), p.8.

14. On the barriers to written expression by people in oppressive situations, see Tillie Olsen, *Silences* (New York: Delta/ Seymour Lawrence, 1978). On differences of expression by social class, see Pierre Bourdieu, *Distinction: A Social Critique of the Judgment of Taste,* trans. Richard Nice (Cambridge, Mass.: Harvard University Press, 1984). On writing about an oral culture, see Julie Cruikshank in collaboration with Angela Sidney, Kitty Smith, and Annie Ned, *Life Lived like a Story: Life Stories of Three Yukon Native Elders* (Vancouver: University of British Columbia Press, 1990), p.19.

15. While commitment to the goals and principles of unionism is healthy, there are clearly toxic patterns in the way many union activists work. For example, see Melody Beattie, *Beyond Codependency and Getting Better All the Time* (New York: Harper and Row, 1989). On the consequences of work worship for personal burnout, see William L. Bryan, "Preventing Burnout in the Public Interest Community," in *Grantsmanship Center News,* Los Angeles, March-April 1981. On the broader cultural currents that reinforce co-dependency, see Juliet B. Schor, *The Overworked American: The Unexpected Decline of Leisure* (New York: Basic Books, 1991).

16. On stress among telephone workers, see Gary Cwitco, "Submission on the

Workers' Compensation Board Discussion Paper on the Compensation of Chronic Occupational Stress," Communications and Electrical Workers of Canada, Toronto, 1989. See also Elia Zurik, Vincent Mosco, and Clarence Lochhead, "Telephone Workers' Reaction to the New Technology," *Industrial Relations/ Relations Industrielles*, Vol.44, No.3 (1989).

17. Most unionists in North America believe that the grievance procedure is an advance over more blunt and spontaneous work stoppages such as those used to settle disputes in most of Western Europe. For the surfacing of doubts on this point, see Michael Lerner, *Surplus Powerlessness* (Oakland, Cal.: Institute for Labor and Mental Health, 1986), p.56.

18. Thomas Walkom, *Rae Days: The Rise and Follies of the NDP* (Toronto: Key Porter, 1994), pp.144–45.

19. Danielle Messia, "De La Main Gauche," in the album *De La Main Gauche* (Paris: Barclay, 1982), trans. Danielle Martin, April 1989.

20. Thinking Union Bulletin, no.1 (September, 1986), Ontario Region, Communications and Electrical Workers of Canada, Toronto.

4. COMING TO TERMS

1. The phrases "badges of ability" and its counterpart "badges of shame" are drawn from Richard Sennett and Jonathan Cobb, *The Hidden Injuries of Class* (New York: Vintage, 1973). The phrase "cracks in consent" came to me through dian marino, a gifted artist and environmental educator. See also James C. Scott, *Domination and the Arts of Resistance: Hidden Transcripts* (New Haven, CT.: Yale University Press, 1990).

2. Alcohol is a powerful presence in union courses and conferences across Canada, not only in the North. The union counselling network has succeeded in creating alcohol-free social rooms in many union events and in holding Alcoholics Anonymous meetings as part of the optional program. Yet the shift from smoke-dominated to smoke-free environments that occurred so rapidly in the late 1980s has yet to extend to alcohol.

3. Sun Tzu, *The Art of War*, trans. Thomas Cleary (Boston: Shambhala/Random House, 1988).

4. The strike is beautifully portrayed from a feminist perspective in Sophie Bissonnette's documentary film *A Wive's Tale* (1983). The tensions between local and district leaders during the strike were similar to those exposed in *The American Dream*, Barbara Kopple's 1991 film about the Hormel strike in the U.S. midwest.

5. James L. Dougherty, *Union Free Management and How to Keep It Free* (Chicago: Dartnell Corporation, 1972).

6. On this point, see "Extension or Communication," in Paulo Freire, *Education for Critical Consciousness* (New York: Seabury Press, 1973).

152

7.   Audrey Lorde, "The Use of Anger: Women Responding to Racism," *Sister, Outsider* (Trumansburg, N.Y.: The Crossing Press, 1984).

8.   Ronald Weihs, *Highball!*, 1979, Unpublished script.

9.   Not his real name.

10. On the shop floor the process during this same period was not always so surgical; see June Corman, "Dissension within the Ranks: The Struggle over Employment Practices," in June Corman, Meg Luxton, D.W. Livingstone, and Wally Seccombe, *Recasting Steel Labour: The Stelco Story* (Halifax: Fernwood Publishing, 1993).

5. CIVIL WAR TIME

1.   A lively account of these events is provided by Ritts, "Cec and Desist," *Hamilton Magazine*, 1987. For a historical perspective, see Bill Freeman, *1005: Political Life in a Union Local* (Toronto: Lorimer, 1982).

2.   Most interesting among those statements was the Communications Policy Statement, which initiated the List-Julien Awards for labour journalism and labour arts. See United Steelworkers of America, "Going Public: The Steelworkers Communications Policy," Canadian Policy Conference, Toronto, 1985.

3.   On fishing, see Silver Donald Cameron, *The Education of Everett Richardson: The Nova Scotia Fishermen's Strike, 1970–71* (Toronto: McClelland and Stewart, 1977); and Sue Calhoun, *A Word to Say: The Story of the Maritime Fishermen's Union* (Halifax: Nimbus Publishing, 1991).

4.   On the economic history of hinterlands, see the "dependency school" theorists such as Samir Amin and Paul Baran. An excellent compilation, including Andre Gunder Frank's seminal "The Development of Underdevelopment," is *The Political Economy of Development and Underdevelopment*, ed. Charles K. Wilber, 3rd ed. (New York: Random House, 1984). Recent applications of this perspective to Canada are found in Tom Naylor's work, and in the compilation *The New Era of Global Competition: State Policy and Market Power*, ed. Daniel Drache and Meric S. Gertler (Montreal and Kingston: McGill-Queen's University Press, 1991).

5.   The economic trap into which Atlantic Canada has been plunged has been the subject of many task forces and inquiries. A consistent critical perspective has been provided by Rick Williams and others, collected in *Toward a New Maritimes*, ed. Ian McKay and Scott Milsom (Charlottetown: Ragweed Press, 1992).

6.   "A Note to Steelworker Friends at the OFL Convention," November 10, 1985.

7.   Freire, *Education for Critical Consciousness*, p.36.

6. BACK TO BASICS:
GRASSROOTS CAMPAIGNS, POWER, AND ART

1. Translated from the Spanish by the author.

2. The academic literature refers to seven kinds of power, and in the situation with the truants all of them seemed to be operating. See Paul Hersey, Kenneth H. Blanchard, and Walter E. Natemeyer, *Situational Leadership, Perception and the Impact of Power* (San Diego, Cal.: Learning Resources Corporation, 1979). This framework of power was introduced to me by Barbara Thomas and Alok Mukherjee, and adapted by them in ways I found useful for my own teaching of local union officers.

3. A labour critique of bias in the arts and media is "expressed in terms of the twin measures of accessibility (or the democratic right of workers to participate in activities which they pay for as taxpayers) and portrayal (or the right of working people to see themselves reflected and respected in the media)." Susan Crean, "Labour Working with Art," *Fuse Magazine*, No.44 (1987), p.30.

4. This campaign is worldwide and of long standing. See, for example, the chilling accounts in Arokia Dass, *Not Beyond Repair: Reflections of a Malaysian Trade Unionist* (Hong Kong: Asia Monitor Resources Centre, 1991).

5. This process was captured in the text of the "photostory" booklet. See Karl Beveridge and Carole Condé, *Class Work* (Toronto: Communications and Electrical Workers of Canada, 1988).

6. The CWC fought the Americanization of Canada that is required for such an agreement to really work in a variety of ways. The union supported the Action Canada Network and the Common Frontiers Program, which linked us up with Mexican counterparts. Some fruits of this work are captured in the booklet published by CEP, "Mexico: Not Quite How We Imagined It," Toronto, 1994.

7. In this section, I draw on a particularly lucid summary by Vincent Mosco to the leadership conference of officers of telephone locals in the Western Region of the CWC, held in Regina, Saskatchewan, April 23, 1991. See also Vincent Mosco, *The Pay-per Society: Computers and Communications in the Information Age* (Toronto: Garamond Press, 1989).

8. Excerpt from Donna Robinson's poem, "Reflections on a Working Life." Donna read her poetry at the first "Woman Talk" session, Mayworks Festival, Toronto, 1988.

9. Laura Sky, speech to "Arts and Labour, Working Partners," a conference sponsored by the Labour Arts and Media Working Group, Labour Council of Metropolitan Toronto, 1983.

7. POLICY TIME ON THE JOB TRAINING FRONT

1. See Robert Kuttner, "The Declining Middle," *Atlantic Monthly*, July 1983. The specific patterns for Canada were best captured in Gordon Betcherman et al.,

Good Jobs, Bad Jobs (Ottawa: Economic Council of Canada, 1989).

2. See Jamie Swift, *Wheel of Fortune: Work and Life in the Age of Falling Expectations* (Toronto: Between the Lines, 1995).

3. David W. Livingstone, "Enterprise Restructuring and New Training Programs: The Challenge for Labour." (Toronto: Ontario Federation of Labour, October 26, 1990), p.12, unpublished.

4. See Kari Dehli, "Subject to the New Global Economy: Power and Positioning in Ontario Labour Market Policy Formulation," *Studies in Political Economy*, No.41 (Summer 1993), p.85, for a discussion of how state efforts to establish new policy-making frameworks for training and education relate to questions of ethnicity, race, gender, sexuality, and (dis)ability.

5. Notes for a luncheon address to "Technology and the Global Economy: An International Policy Conference," Montreal, sponsored by Industry, Science and Technology Canada, in co-operation with other Canadian government departments and agencies and the Organization for Economic Co-operation and Development, February 4, 1991.

6. Ruth Groff, "Worker-Driven Training: A Research Report," CEP, Toronto, 1993.

7. The major exceptions to this pattern, in the construction trade unions, had bought into trust funds and apprenticeship advisory committees, whose scope was limited and dynamic exclusionary, particularly to women.

8. Bill Irwin, Middlesex Federation of Agriculture, presentation to the Consultation Panel for Local Boards, London, Ont., April 1992.

9. See Judy Steed, "No Consensus on Job-Training Scheme: Getting Experimental Partnership Together 'Nightmare on Wheels,'" *The Toronto Star*, July 16, 1993, p.A23.

10. Ontario Federation of Labour, "Education and Training," policy paper, Toronto, November 1991.

8. MERGER TIME

1. The conventional image of "unionist" is of a white man, middle-aged, employed full-time in a stable, industrial job. But this image is already a generation behind the social diversity of today's unions. See in particular White, *Sisters and Solidarity*.

2. Paulo Freire, *Pedagogy of the Oppressed* (New York: Herder and Herder, 1971), p.58.

3. That such initiatives seek enhanced productivity is obvious enough. The question is what opportunities this creates for unions. Among the optimists would be Andy Banks and Jack Metzgar, "Participating in Management: Union Organizing on a New Terrain," *Labor Research Review* (Chicago: Midwest Center for Labor Research, 1989). Among the pessimists would be Don Wells, *Soft Sell:*

`Quality of Working Life' Programs and the Productivity Race* (Ottawa: Canadian Centre for Policy Alternatives, 1986).

4. John Edwards, internal correspondence reproduced with permission, September 1993.

9. FUTURE TENSE:
DISCIPLINARY DILEMMAS AND MOVEMENT BUILDING

1. No doubt my actions on the question of dress have been somewhat arbitrary, even silly. Yet serious issues remain about how our daily practices embody a stance in regard to cultural capital. For more systematic approaches to analysing and quantifying cultural capital, see Bourdieu, *Distinction*, pp.80–91.

2. Sun Tzu, *Art of War*, p.6.

3. The level of sophistication of Swedish unions in dealing with these matters is rather overwhelming for a Canadian unionist. See, for example, the vision for humanized work presented in Swedish National Public/ State Employees' Union, "Both Head and Hand: A Job for People: Our Goal for the 90's," Stockholm, 1989.

4. Sobel and Meurer, *Working at Inglis*.

5. See Rick Arnold, Bev Burke, Carl James, D'Arcy Martin, and Barb Thomas, *Educating for a Change* (Toronto: Doris Marshall Institute and Between the Lines, 1991).

6. I have been helped in this area greatly by participants in a Process Consultation course at the Faculty of Environmental Studies, York University, from 1991 to 1994.

7. I was helped greatly in this area by participants in a therapy group led by Mardi Goodman-Thomas, from 1990 to 1993.

SELECTED BIBLIOGRAPHY

■ ■ ■ ■

The notes for each chapter provide some of the sources used in the writing of this book. What follows is a selection of easily available sources that have influenced my general approach. I've identified ten of them (■) as key references for readers who want to learn more about the Canadian labour movement; and I have provided a few words of annotation for this "top ten."

Argue, Robert, Charlene Gannage, and David Livingstone. 1987. *Working People and Hard Times*. Toronto: Garamond Press.

Arnold, Rick, Bev Burke, Carl James, D'Arcy Martin, and Barb Thomas. 1991. *Educating for a Change*. Toronto: Doris Marshall Institute and Between the Lines.

■ Barna, Laszlo and Laura Alper. 1982. *Who Wants Unions?* Montreal: National Film Board of Canada. Video.
  • A visit of 27 minutes with Charles Hughes, a leading American advocate of union-free management, with some comment on the economic and social effects of his approach.

Betcherman, Gordon et al. 1989. *Good Jobs, Bad Jobs*. Ottawa: Economic Council of Canada.

Briskin, Linda and Patricia McDermott. 1993. *Women Challenging Unions: Feminism, Democracy and Militancy*. Toronto: University of Toronto Press.

■ Bush, Steven and Allen Booth. 1984. *Life on the Line*. Toronto: Playwrights Canada.
  • The script for an insightful and poetic one-person play on unemployment.

Calhoun, Sue. 1991. *A Word to Say: The Story of the Maritime Fishermen's Union*. Halifax: Nimbus Publishing.

- Cameron, Silver Donald. 1977. *The Education of Everett Richardson: The Nova Scotia Fishermen's Strike, 1970–71*. Toronto: McClelland and Stewart.
  - A vivid account of the bitter struggle by Nova Scotia fishermen for union recognition and economic justice.

Canadian Labour Congress. 1986. *The Steward Handbook*. Ottawa: CLC.

Canadian Labour Market and Productivity Centre. 1990. *Labour Research Resource Manual*. Ottawa: CLMPC.

- Condé, Carole and Karl Beveridge. 1986. *First Contract: Women and the Fight to Unionize*. Toronto: Between the Lines.
  - A photostory based on the Steelworkers' organizing drive among the women working in the Radio Shack warehouse in Barrie, Ontario, in the late 1970s. Beautifully produced colour photomontages by these well-known labour artists.

Corman, June, Meg Luxton, D.W. Livingstone, and Wally Seccombe. 1993. *Recasting Steel Labour: The Stelco Story*. Halifax: Fernwood Publishing.

- Cornish, Mary and Lynn Spink. 1994. *Organizing Unions*. Toronto: Second Story Press.
  - A clear, practical handbook for workers wanting to unionize, with sample legal documents and detailed procedures for the campaign, vote, and first contract.

Daly, Herman E. and John B. Cobb. 1989. *For the Common Good: Redirecting the Economy Toward Community, the Environment and a Sustainable Future*. Boston: Beacon Press.

Dass, Arokia. 1991. *Not Beyond Repair: Reflections of a Malaysian Trade Unionist*. Hong Kong: Asia Monitor Resource Centre.

Dunk, Thomas W. 1991. *It's a Working Man's Town: Male Working-Class Culture in Northwestern Ontario*. Montreal and Kingston: McGill-Queen's University Press.

Freire, Paulo and Ira Shor. 1987. *A Pedagogy for Liberation: Dialogues on Transforming Education*. Westport, CT: Bergin and Garvey.

Golden, Miriam and Jonas Pontusson, eds. 1992. *Bargaining for Change: Union Politics in North America and Europe*. Ithaca, N.Y.: Cornell University Press.

Gramsci, Antonio. 1971. *Selections from the Prison Notebooks*, ed. Quintin Hoare and G. Nowell-Smith. New York: International Publications.

Hart, Mechthild U. 1992. *Working and Educating for Life: Feminist and International Perspectives on Adult Education*. London: Routledge.

Heron, Craig, Shea Hoffmitz, Wayne Roberts, and Robert Storey. 1981. *All That Our Hands Have Done: A Pictorial History of the Hamilton Workers*. Oakville, Ont.: Mosaic Press.

- Heron, Craig. 1989. *The Canadian Labour Movement: A Short History*. Toronto: James Lorimer and Company.
  - The clearest introduction available, from a left perspective, to the struggles

that have shaped work, the working class, and the labour movement in Canada.

Karasek, Robert and Tores Theorell. 1990. *Healthy Work: Stress, Productivity and the Reconstruction of Working Life*. New York: Basic Books.

Lerner, Michael. 1986. *Surplus Powerlessness*. Oakland, Cal.: Institute for Labor and Mental Health.

Levine, Philip. 1984. *Selected Poems*. New York: Atheneum.

▪ Mackay, Claire. 1987. *Pay Cheques and Picket Lines: All About Unions in Canada*. Toronto: Kids Can Press.

  • A lovely introduction to the labour movement, for young people aged 10–15. Filled with anecdotes, humour, and good visual design.

Mantle, Arlene. 1989. *Class Act*. Toronto: On the Line Music Collective. Audio cassette.

Marshall, Judith, with Domingos Chigarire, Helena Francisco, Antonio Goncalves, and Leonardo Nhantumbo. 1990. *Training for Empowerment: A Kit of Materials Based on an Exchange among Literacy Workers in Mozambique, Brazil and Nicaragua*. Toronto: International Council for Adult Education and Doris Marshall Institute.

Mosco, Vincent. 1989. *The Pay-per Society: Computers and Communications in the Information Age*. Toronto: Garamond Press.

Ontario Federation of Labour. 1989. "Education and Training." Policy Document No.5, 33rd annual convention, November.

Ontario Federation of Labour. 1993. "Towards a Living Culture." Policy Document No.6, 2nd biennial convention, November.

Ontario Workers Arts and Heritage Centre. 1993. *All We Worked For.* Video.

Panitch, Leo and Donald Swartz. 1985. *From Consent to Coercion: The Assault on Trade Union Freedoms*. Toronto: Garamond Press.

Park, Peter, Mary Brydon-Miller, Budd Hall, and Ted Jackson. 1993. *Voices of Change: Participatory Research in the United States and Canada*. Toronto: OISE Press.

Parker, Mike and Jane Slaughter. 1990. *Choosing Sides: Unions and the Team Concept*. Detroit: Labor Notes/ South End Press.

Prieur, Deborah and Mary Rowles. 1992. *Taking Action: A Union Guide to Ending Violence against Women*. Vancouver: B.C. Federation of Labour and Women's Research Centre.

Razack, Sherene. 1993. "Storytelling for Social Change," in *Returning the Gaze: Essays on Racism, Feminism and Politics*, ed. Himani Bannerji. Toronto: Sister Vision Press.

Reagon, Bernice Johnson. 1983. "Coalition Politics: Turning the Century" in *Home Girls: A Black Feminist Anthology*, ed. Barbara Smith. Latham, NY: Kitchen Table/ Women of Color Press.

Rich, Adrienne. 1991. *An Atlas of the Difficult World: Poems 1988–91*. New York: Norton.

Rose, Jeff. 1991. *Worth Fighting For: Selected Speeches and Articles, 1983–91.* Ottawa: Canadian Union of Public Employees.

Sennett, Richard and Jonathan Cobb. 1973. *The Hidden Injuries of Class.* New York: Vintage.

Seymour, Edward. 1974. *An Illustrated History of Canadian Labour.* Ottawa: Canadian Labour Congress.

Shedden, Leslie. 1983. *Mining Photographs and Other Pictures, 1948–68.* Sydney, N.S.: University College of Cape Breton Press/ Nova Scotia School of Art and Design.

Sinclair, Jim, ed. 1992. *Crossing the Line: Canada and Free Trade With Mexico.* Vancouver: New Star Books.

Smith, Doug. 1985. *Let Us Rise! An Illustrated History of the Manitoba Labour Movement.* Vancouver: New Star Books.

■ Sobel, David and Susan Meurer. 1994. *Working at Inglis: The Life and Death of a Canadian Factory.* Toronto: James Lorimer and Company.

• A careful and comprehensive portrait of a Toronto factory, which captures many of the patterns of Canadian industrial life. Thoroughly researched and always respectful of the workers who are portrayed and quoted.

Steedman, Mercedes, Peter Suschnigg, and Dieter K. Buse. 1995. *Hard Lessons: The Mine Mill Union in the Canadian Labour Movement.* Toronto: Dundurn Press.

Sun Tzu. 1963. *The Art of War.* Trans. Thomas Cleary. Boston: Random House/ Shambhala.

■ Swift, Jamie. 1995. *Wheel of Fortune: Work and Life in the Age of Falling Expectations.* Toronto: Between the Lines.

• A persuasive, if somewhat chilling, journey through the new economy from the perspective of working people. A vivid and passionate account, which balances everyday life with overall structural analysis.

Thomas, Alan M. 1991. *Beyond Education: A New Perspective on Society's Management of Learning.* San Francisco: Jossey-Bass.

Turk, Jim, ed. 1989. "It's Our Own Knowledge: Labour, Public Education and Skills Training." Special issue of *Our Schools/ Our Selves*, Vol.1, No.8.

Wagner, Jane. 1987. *The Search for Signs of Intelligent Life in the Universe.* New York: Harper and Row.

Walker, George F. 1984. *Criminals in Love.* Toronto: Playwrights Canada.

Wayman, Tom. 1986. *The Face of Jack Munro.* Vancouver: Left Bank Publishing.

■ White, Julie. 1993. *Sisters and Solidarity: Women and Unions in Canada.* Toronto: Thompson Educational Publishing.

• A matter-of-fact review of progress and setbacks for women active in the labour movement. Clear, informative, and useful to those who feel that feminism and unionism need to negotiate the terms of alliance.

White, Robert. 1987. *Hard Bargains: My Life on the Line.* Toronto: McClelland and Stewart.

PICTURE CREDITS

■ ■ ■ ■